DIVORCE AND REMARRIAGE
IN THE CATHOLIC CHURCH

DIVORCE AND REMARRIAGE
IN THE
CATHOLIC CHURCH

edited by

Lawrence G. Wrenn

NEWMAN PRESS
New York / Paramus / Toronto

Library of Congress
Catalog Card Number: 73-75744

ISBN 0-8091-1769-X (paper)
ISBN 0-8091-0183-1 (cloth)

Published by Newman Press
Editorial Office: 1865 Broadway, N.Y., N.Y. 10023
Business Office: 400 Sette Drive, Paramus, N.J. 07652

Printed and bound in the
United States of America

CONTENTS

Foreword

It is likely that the title of this book will startle some, engage the curiosity of others and, lamentably, cause the book to be dismissed unread by those who will suppose it to contain yet another proposal for radical change in a Church they consider to be changeless. But the title should not startle. Divorce and remarriage have been recognized and approved in the Catholic Church for a very long time. Contemporary interest in the matter among theologians, biblicists, canonists, sociologists, and philosophers is not centered on *whether* the Catholic Church can or should allow remarriage after divorce, but rather *in what circumstances* should the Church do so.

Remarriage after separation from a valid prior marriage was allowed in the primitive Church in certain circumstances which constituted an obstacle to one's embracing and living the Christian faith; this has commonly been referred to as the Pauline privilege. This "privilege of the faith," which took precedence over the natural permanence of marriage, was later extended to situations not encompassed by the original Pauline teaching. Remarriage has also long been allowed after the failure of a prior marriage which, though valid and even sacramental, was not consummated.

These instances of Catholic endorsement of divorce and remarriage have come under intensive study in these tumultuous days of rethinking and renewal with a view to discovering if the principles involved can be applied to other, analogous situations. It is neither the purpose nor the necessary effect of such studies to weaken respect for the element of permanence in Christian marriage. It is their purpose, rather, to deepen the Church's understanding of this permanence, its true nature, origin and meaning, and its relationship to other values inherent in Christian marriage; and it is scarcely to be regretted that the effect of such studies has been to awaken hope in the hearts of many Catholics who have remarried after divorce and for whom no realistic possibility of ecclesial reconciliation presently exists.

Among the most dedicated servants of the people of God are those who staff the Church's matrimonial tribunals. Not only must they process the difficult cases in which *dissolution* of a marriage is sought on one of the grounds referred to above, but also the far greater number of cases in which what is sought is *annulment*—a declaration that an apparently valid prior marriage was in fact null and void from the beginning. Often hampered by cumbersome procedures, legal technicalities, shortage of personnel and uncooperative witnesses, tribunal staffs struggle to reconcile the reality of divorce and remarriage with the Church's constant concern to preserve the values of permanence in marriage. Much has been done in the past decade to improve tribunal procedures, and much jurisprudence has evolved regarding sufficient grounds for declarations of nullity. Yet it remains the concern of many, within and without tribunals, that the Church's present approaches to the matter of divorce and remarriage are needlessly stringent, excessively legal, and insensitive to contemporary sociological and theological insights.

This study originated in a resolution of the Canon Law Society of America gathered in Convention in New Orleans in 1970. It was my honor, while President of that Society, to appoint Lawrence G. Wrenn to direct the project. The choice of Father Wrenn was based, in part, on his own years of tribunal experience (which have yielded his celebrated publication *Annulments,* now in its second edition), in part on his widely recognized devotion and loyalty to the Church, its teachings and its institutions, and in part on his possessing that kind of love for the Church which impels him to strive to remove from it what seems to him to be its imperfections. Not only his leadership in gathering this collection of essays, but the quality of his own contribution in the final chapter is ample vindication of that choice.

Robert T. Kennedy

St. Joseph's Seminary
Yonkers, New York
February 12, 1973

George W. MacRae, S.J.

New Testament Perspectives on Marriage and Divorce

No reader will expect to find in the New Testament a justification for or a critique of the institution of marriage tribunals. To seek one would be an exercise in anachronism, if not wrongheadedness. In addition, however, it would be theologically naive to conclude that therefore the tribunals have no justification in the life of the Church. For just as a good deal of recent theological literature has reminded us that we cannot expect to find the institution of priesthood in the New Testament and yet should not therefore regard priesthood as itself in question,[1] there is an analogy with many other features of the Church's structure, thought and practice. The Church must be constantly aware of its "home" in the New Testament communities and the teaching of Jesus; it must indeed be subject to the judgment of Scripture in all that it says and does. But even the Church "can't go home again." It cannot solve problems of its own time and culture by a flight into the past of its beginnings, which are often rather romantically portrayed.[2]

In fact, there is a surprising amount of material in the New Testament, especially in the Pauline correspondence, which indirectly supports the development of such institutions as the marriage tribunal. St. Paul urged the Corinthian community more than once to regulate its own affairs. In the case of the incestuous man (1 Cor 5) he ordered the Corinthians uncompromisingly to take drastic action to protect the integrity—including the moral integrity—of the community by "excommunicating" the offender. In the next chapter of the same epistle he rebuked the community for its failure to deal with lawsuits in "courts" of its own making: "Do you not know that the saints will judge the world?"

The case of the lawsuits is an interesting analogy for the business of marriage tribunals, although traditionally Catholic theology has been reluctant to seek analogies to its teaching on marriage and divorce. In 1 Corinthians 6:1-11 the genuine Christian stance is not to have lawsuits with one another in the first place. But when they exist—and Paul is no less a realist than Canon Law—the community has the competence to deal with them. It is true that in the same epistle Paul also discusses marriage and divorce—and we must return to the passage presently—but in that context he makes no provision for any quasi-juridical determinations on the part of the Church. The point here is not really whether one can find some biblical precedent for the marriage tribunal, nor whether Paul would have felt more or less at home with our modern tribunals, but rather that the Pauline "Church order" allows for the Church taking the responsibility, even formally and almost institutionally, for the management of its own affairs. I should like later to suggest an analogous function for the marriage tribunals, which I do not think they now feel empowered to perform.

But the main issue I wish to raise in these pages is not whether we look to the New Testament when examining our modern ecclesiastical life. One may hope we will do so increasingly as a theology and an ecclesiastical "life-style" for our age continue to be elaborated. Rather, the issue is: What do we look for when we turn to the New Testament and the teaching of Jesus? Do we seek the formulation of an absolute, divinely revealed law or model, or do we seek a process of understanding and adaptation with which the modern Church can identify only by entering into the process and furthering it? I believe it is the latter that is the more appropriate by virtue of the nature of the New Testament materials themselves. I should like to illustrate this choice and develop the principles involved by examining the New Testament statements on the indissolubility of marriage. Obviously the example chosen is one that is of considerable concern to the marriage tribunals, though it does not directly determine their propriety or utility. As much as possible, these pages will deal with the New Testament question and the issues to which it gives rise, avoiding facile comparisons and contrasts with later Church practice. On the other hand, we will try to avoid becoming mired in exegetical detail and conjecture; in this question more than many others exegetical ingenuity has obscured what is really present in the New Testament itself.

What God Has Joined Together

Information about Jesus' teaching on the indissolubility of marriage comes to us from three main sources: (1) the Gospel of Mark, which I take to be the earliest extant example of the genre Gospel;[3] (2) Q, the sayings collection drawn upon apparently independently by both Matthew and Luke; and (3) Paul's tradition about the sayings of the Lord. These sources are preserved for us in the five New Testament passages (Mk 10:2-12 and Mt 19:3-12; Lk 16:18 and Mt 5:32; 1 Cor 7:10-16) which have always been the object of intense study on the part of theologians and biblical scholars but which lately have unleashed a flood of literature.[4] It is remarkable that no single interpretation of these passages has ever won what could be called the general consent of interpreters, at least of Catholic ones, and the Church has reflected this hesitancy by never attempting to define their sense. It is not the intention of these pages to survey this mass of scholarship or to build upon any argument from consensus. Instead, the very diversity of interpretation suggests a tendency to resist the obvious implications of these passages. Let us examine them in succession.

1. The Markan version of the saying of Jesus places it in the context of a challenge from the Pharisees (10:2), though a somewhat obscure one, since in asking whether divorce was allowed, they were supposedly ignoring the explicit provision of the Torah (Dt 24:1). Jesus makes them cite the Torah passage and then he interprets it as a concession to hard-heartedness. Jesus' own reflections center on the order of creation: he cites Genesis 1:27 and 2:24 and comments: "What therefore God has joined together, let not man put asunder" (10:9). Privately, as elsewhere in the Gospel,[5] his disciples question him about his statement and Jesus replies: "Whoever divorces his wife and marries another, commits adultery against her; and if she divorces her husband and marries another, she commits adultery" (10:11-12).

The original force of Jesus' encounter with the Pharisees is lost in Mark's version, and the whole passage is very typical of that Gospel in structure. Moreover, the form of Jesus' interpretation of his own words is difficult to imagine in a Palestinian-Jewish (in contrast to a Roman) setting where the concept of a woman divorcing her husband was unheard of —unless we are to imagine that Jesus consciously wished to extend the individual responsibility in marriage to the wife as well.[6] In any event, the point of the saying is clear: Jesus unequivocally and unconditionally rules out divorce.

The Matthean version of this incident is much more coherent, but in view of Matthew's habitual treatment of his Markan source, it is not therefore more original, as has sometimes been alleged.[7] In Matthew the Pharisees put Jesus to the test by inviting him to take sides in a famous Jewish legal dispute: "Is it lawful to divorce one's wife *for any cause?*" (19:3). The issue is that between the school of Shammai, for whom divorce was permissible only on the grounds of adultery, and the school of Hillel, for whom divorce was permissible on many grounds. The surprising thing is that at least at first sight, after resisting the trap with his interpretation of Genesis, Jesus then seems to fall into it, for his saying on divorce is addressed to the Pharisees, not to the disciples, and it contains the famous exceptive clause: "And I say to you: whoever divorces his wife, *except for unchastity (mē epi porneia)*, and marries another, commits adultery" (19:9). Perhaps it is only Matthew's concern for interpreting the teaching of Jesus within his own community that leads him to make Jesus' position seem not sufficiently distinct from that of Shammai. That is to say, the dynamic of the encounter with the Pharisees is less important to Matthew than the practical implementation of Jesus' teaching in the community. More on this in a moment. Let us forego, at least for the present, all the philological discussion which centuries of exegetes have found irresistible. It is enough to note that no matter how the exceptive clause is to be interpreted,[8] it seems to reflect a modification within the Matthean community of the absoluteness of Jesus' prohibition.

2. The Lukan witness to the saying (16:18) is completely independent of the discussion with the Pharisees in which Matthew and Mark place it. For convenience we regard the Lukan verse as derived from the Q source, conscious that this derivation could be challenged since the Matthean parallel in the Sermon on the Mount is not a close one. In Luke, the context contributes almost nothing to the understanding of the saying; it is best treated as an isolated element of Jesus' teaching and is often regarded as the clearest and most "primitive" form of the tradition: "Everyone who divorces his wife and marries another commits adultery, and he who marries a woman divorced from her husband commits adultery."

Another Matthean witness to the saying (5:32)—whether derived from Q or a Matthean reworking of the Markan story —presents the same problem as Matthew 19:9. Here the context is the Sermon on the Mount and specifically the list of antitheses between what was said in the Torah and the demands of Christian righteousness. In contrast to the law in

Deuteronomy 24:1 Jesus says: "But I say to you that everyone who divorces his wife, *except on the ground of unchastity* (*parektos logou porneias*), makes her an adulteress; and whoever marries a divorced woman commits adultery."

3. For a number of reasons it may be suggested that the most important New Testament passage on the indissolubility of marriage is Paul's discussion of it in 1 Corinthians 7. This is chronologically the earliest witness both to a traditional saying of the Lord and to the practice of the early Christian communities. And like Matthew, Paul too both reiterates an absolute doctrine and introduces a qualification. And like Mark, Paul expresses the prohibition in terms of the mutual obligations of husband and wife, though without implying complete equality. In fact, in Paul's statement there is no linguistic allusion whatever to the Synoptic sayings, but this is not surprising when we note that Paul gives this teaching as his own even though he understands it to coincide with that of Jesus: "To the married I give charge, not I but the Lord, that the wife should not separate from her husband (but if she does, let her remain single or else be reconciled to her husband)—and that the husband should not divorce [9] his wife" (7:10-11).

Having addressed "the married (Christians)," Paul immediately turns to "the rest," i.e., those in "mixed marriages," presumably marriages in which one partner has subsequently become Christian. In this instance, Paul speaks on his own authority: "To the rest I say, not the Lord . . ." (7:12); but there is no indication that his strictures are less authoritative here. First, he forbids the Christian partner in such a union to initiate divorce, "for the unbelieving husband is consecrated through his wife, and the unbelieving wife is consecrated through her husband" (7:14). But secondly, he asserts the freedom of the Christian partner in cases where the non-Christian partner initiates divorce: "But if the unbelieving partner desires to separate, let it be so; in such a case the brother or sister is not bound.[10] For God has called us to peace" (7:15). This is the precedent for what became the classic case of the "Pauline privilege" in later Church practice. For our purposes it is enough to note at present that Paul on his own authority admits an "exception" to the indissolubility of marriage—which, to be sure, he understands as primarily applicable to the Christian situation, but also to the mixed as far as the Christian's initiative is concerned.

Let Not Man Put Asunder

What is the total impact of the New Testament evidence about the absolute indissolubility of marriage? First, all three of our sources (Mark, Q and Paul) report an unqualified prohibition of divorce as a saying of Jesus. The only reasonable conclusion is that this is what Jesus really taught. It could not reasonably be accounted for as an invention of the early Church because it so radically runs counter to the accepted practice of both Jewish and Greco-Roman society. One should note that the method underlying this conclusion is not the mathematical analogy of the least common denominator but the careful analysis of the development of the forms of dominical sayings in the Synoptic tradition.[11] In the overall context of the preaching of Jesus this radical and uncompromising assertion must be seen in relation to the eschatological urgency of his preaching: the kingdom of God is at hand!

Our second observation on the basis of the above survey of passages is that, of the four New Testament authors who deal with the teaching of Jesus about marriage and divorce, two of them make exceptions to the absolute statement. It is this fact which must be reckoned with, not by any exegetical legerdemain, but by attempting to understand the process by which the sayings of Jesus were evaluated and transmitted in the New Testament itself. That we are really dealing with exceptions on the part of Matthew (or his community) and Paul becomes clear if we allow the texts to say what they most obviously seem to say. Let us first eliminate some unsuccessful attempts to avoid this conclusion.

One cannot introduce into the New Testament the distinction between a sacramental marriage and a non-sacramental marriage. In the Synoptic passages there is no hint of the possible sacramentality of marriage. On the contrary, the argument for the indissolubility of marriage in the Markan source is derived from the order of creation and thus makes no special provision for the Christian believer at all. Paul, on the other hand, seems at first sight to place Christian marriage in a separate category, but this is not really so, for the point of his concentration is the attitude of the Christian partner, not the nature of the marriage itself. From the point of view of the Christian, a marriage entered into before conversion is as "permanent" as one between Christians. It is not the nature of the marriage which determines its permanence, but the commitment of the partners. The Christian partner who is "deserted," i.e., divorced, is "not bound." It is important to emphasize the fact that it is reading Christian history backward to argue that the New Testament is even "implicitly" talking about the distinction between sacramental and non-sacramental marriage which the later Church articulated. What is most significant is that the later Church is responsible for this distinction, not any revealed divine law. And if the Church is responsible, it is our suggestion here that the Church is empowered to modify the distinction if it should see fit to do so. The nature of marriage as derived from the early Church's understanding of the order of creation is apparently not so absolute as to exclude all exceptions.

Again, one cannot argue that the exceptive clauses of Matthew or the Pauline exception have to do with separation without the right to remarry. If the context of Matthew is a Jewish (-Christian) one, such an arrangement is simply meaningless. As for the situation of 1 Corinthians 7, it is true that Paul explicitly rules out remarriage in the first case that he deals with, that of Christian partners initiating separation. It is probably also true that, given his eschatological perspective, Paul would dissuade the divorced Christian partner of a mixed marriage from remarrying (cf. 1 Cor 7:8, 27). But he makes it unequivocally clear in the same context that those who are free, i.e., widows and those who have never been married, do no wrong, even in the situation of a proximate eschatological expectation, if they choose to marry (cf. 1 Cor 7:9, 28, 39). It is very difficult to imagine him holding an unexpressed reservation for the victims of a broken marriage whom he expressly calls "not bound."

One could continue to list and criticize attempts to read the New Testament passages in such a way that they do not conflict with traditional Church practice. But the longer the list, the more uncomfortable we become about the very presuppositions of such attempts. Instead, we should perhaps look to the larger contexts of the preaching of Jesus, Paul and Matthew and seek to identify the factors which the early Christians understood to authorize them to interpret the teaching of Jesus without abandoning it.

It has already been pointed out that the context of Jesus' radical reinterpretation of the law was an eschatological one. Paul had certainly not lost that sense of eschatological urgency when writing 1 Corinthians 7, but Paul confronted a new situation which had not been part of Jesus' experience. He is conscious of the newness of the situation and of the lack of direct guidance from the Lord when he points out that the instruction on mixed marriages is his own. A few verses later this consciousness is even more emphatic: "Now concerning the unmarried, I have no command of the Lord, but I give my opinion as one who by the Lord's mercy is trustworthy" (7:25). The new situation is the missionary one in which Christians are confronted with working out a way to live in the midst of pagan society. Paul does not abandon the lofty ideal of the dominical teaching about marriage; he repeats it (7:10-11). But he accommodates it to the new situation of mixed marriages, in effect introducing an exception to the absolute indissolubility of marriage. By what authority? He ends the discussion of marriage and celibacy with the remark, "And I think that I have the Spirit of God" (7:40b).

Matthew too faces a new situation with respect to the teaching of Jesus, which he too first reaffirms (19:6). The eschatological message of the pressing kingdom of heaven has now to be related to the on-going life of a Jewish-Christian Church, a Church which is confronted with solving the daily problems of its existence by exercising the powers of binding and loosing.[12] In this context Matthew—or the community he represents—is empowered by his understanding of Jesus' intentions to adapt his teaching on marriage to a situation in which a marriage broken by "unchastity" can no longer be understood as a marriage. It is of course *possible* that *porneia* in the Matthean exceptive clauses refers to a marriage within degrees of kindred which Gentiles might tolerate but Jews (i.e., Jewish Christians) would regard as incestuous (Lev 18: 7-18).[13] Such a marriage would be intolerable in the eyes of Matthew's community. But that is by no means the obvious meaning of the passage since it is not clear that such a union would be regarded as a marriage in the first place. It is at least equally understandable in a Jewish-Christian context that adultery would in fact establish the situation of a ruptured marital union that was once genuine.[14]

What we must suppose in the Matthean Church is a conflict of values that has to be resolved in the on-going life of the Church and for which the tradition about Jesus' sayings provides no immediately applicable solution. The confrontation is between the principle of the indissolubility of marriage which is the tradition of Jesus' teaching and the "right" to a genuine integral marriage. The latter would no doubt be more deeply felt in a community of Jewish background where marriage was regarded as a duty.[15] If Matthew's solution falls into something like the Shammaite interpretation of the Torah which Jesus had avoided in the controversy story, we must allow that the inconsistency may mean much more to the modern interpreter than to a Jewish-Christian community of the late first century.[16] The interpretation of Shammai was not a rabbinic innovation, after all, but a strict construction of the law itself in Deuteronomy 24:1.

God Has Called Us to Peace

It is time to draw some conclusions and formulate some suggestions regarding the status of New Testament teaching on the indissolubility of marriage and the status of contemporary Church practice.

First, regarding the teaching of Jesus. We have indicated above that we can with some confidence identify what was Jesus' attitude toward divorce and what was that of some of the New Testament writers, and these are not identical. It would be false to conclude that theological judgment must rest on our ability, through historical and literary means, to isolate Jesus' teaching at the expense of that of his followers. In the light of modern New Testament scholarship, especially the methods of source, form and redaction criticism applied to the Gospels, there is widespread agreement among interpreters that we have access to the mind of Jesus primarily —indeed only—through the interpretation of the early Christian communities and their theologians. The authority of Jesus' teaching does not reach us independently of the Church. Consequently we cannot assume, in view of the role of Scripture in the life of the Church, that what scholarly research points to as Jesus' own utterance is necessarily any more determinative for the Church than what are apparently the interpretations of him by his followers. This means that we cannot regard as more authoritative for Church life the apparently "primitive" Lukan form of the divorce statement rather than the qualified Matthean form.

On another level, this observation means that we cannot rest Church practice regarding marriage and divorce upon a supposedly divine revealed law—to the extent that the New

Testament serves as the vehicle of that revelation. Instead we must discern the process by which the teaching of Jesus was remembered, communicated, interpreted, adapted and enshrined in the practice of the early Christian communities. That process, we have seen, is one of accommodation to circumstances that were not the context of the preaching of Jesus himself. The Church of today must relate, not to an absolute divine law which is in practice inaccessible to our scholarly research, but to the process of identifying what is of Christ and what is Christian and entering into that discerning process for our own day. The matrix of modern discernment is, as it was in the churches of Paul or Matthew, the dwelling of the Holy Spirit among God's people.

But Jesus did teach the absolute indissolubility of marriage (note that the New Testament does not authorize us to say "of *Christian* marriage"). Was his teaching then merely an ideal from which the "realist" perceives an inevitable decline? There are modern authors who stress the nature of Jesus' matrimonial teaching as an ideal.[17] If we have in mind the formulation of Matthew 5:32, especially in the context of the antitheses of the Sermon on the Mount, there are good grounds for this view.[18] Nor does this mean the "reduction" of the Sermon on the Mount to a mere statement of an impossible ideal over against a serious program for a Christian morality.[19] The alternative of law vs. ideal is not a complete disjunction; there is also what some theologians call "Gospel," the genuine and specifically Christian challenge that can only be met by the fusion of free will and grace. But perhaps one can and even must go a step further and argue that the very preservation of the teaching of Jesus in all its eschatological and challenging purity *requires* the kind of adaptation the early Christians made.[20] The paradox is not meant to be a logical statement but an existential one. What prevents Jesus' teaching from becoming a chimera is the willingness to interpret it anew in each generation. And in this respect, is there not a serious danger that an intransigent interpretation of

the indissolubility of marriage in the Catholic Church today
is rapidly approaching the point of disdain for the ideal itself
as a utopian one?

But are there in fact grounds for the discernment of new
situations in the life of modern Christians which require new
interpretation and new adaptation of the New Testament teaching on marriage? An ever growing number of serious theologians
and Christian social scientists believe that there are. It would far
outstrip the present writer's competence to attempt to describe
these factors, but the reader may simply be referred to the other
chapters in this book. What is emerging is a new perception of
values, and every age of creative thought must perceive its own
values anew. There is a growing consciousness of the conflict
of values in our Christian society over the issue of marriage, the
conflict between a clear but inflexible matrimonial legislation
which does indeed express an important part of the Christian
ethical ideal, and a way of life that must reflect Christian love,
pardon, dedication and self-giving in a world of loveless tech-
nocracy and existential depression.

The marriage tribunal was our starting point. What are we
to conclude about it? If its principal function is a judicial
one, modeled on the kind of civil judiciary that St. Paul ex-
coriated the Corinthians for having recourse to, then it has
no place in the life of the Church. The Church is a human
society and its agencies are human agencies, but it is not a
civil society and its courts are not civil courts. But if the
tribunal can be modified so that it really enters into the process of discerning values and narrowing the perennial gap between Christian ideals and the practice of Christians, then
it has an important role to play. It must arbitrate a conflict
of values, not a conflict of laws. But the courts are interpreters of the law. In that case, the Church's tribunals have
but one law to serve, what St. Paul calls the "law of Christ":
"If a man is overtaken in any trespass, you who are spiritual
should restore him in a spirit of gentleness. . . . Bear one another's burdens, and so fulfill the law of Christ" (Gal 6:1-2).

NOTES

1. See, e.g., R. E. Brown, *Priest and Bishop, Biblical Reflections* (New York: Paulist Press, 1970); H. Küng, *Why Priests?* (Garden City: Doubleday, 1972).

2. Only after writing the above paragraph did I read R. L. Wilken, *The Myth of Christian Beginnings* (Garden City: Doubleday, 1971), which develops eloquently the argument implied in the adoption of Thomas Wolfe's title.

3. It would not be appropriate here to substantiate the use of the so-called two-source theory of Synoptic relationships, which a majority of Catholic scholars now seem to accept. For a recent discussion, see J. A. Fitzmyer, "The Priority of Mark and the 'Q' Source in Luke," in *Jesus and Man's Hope* I (Pittsburgh: Pittsburgh Theological Seminary, 1970), pp. 131-170.

4. Much of it quite independent of the recent divorce question in Italian civil law. For bibliography see J. Dupont, *Mariage et Divorce dans l'Évangile* (Bruges: Desclée de Brouwer, 1959); B. Vawter, "The Divorce Clauses in Mt 5, 32 and 19, 9," in *Catholic Biblical Quarterly* 16 (1954), pp. 155-167; D. L. Dungan, *The Sayings of Jesus in the Churches of Paul* (Philadelphia: Fortress Press, 1971), pp. 83-131; and for some suggestions on the most recent literature, cf. L. Sabourin, "The Divorce Clauses (Mt 5:32; 19:9)," in *Biblical Theology Bulletin* 2 (1972), pp. 80-86.

5. Notably in the interpretation of parables: 4:10; 7:17.

6. Contrast Paul's conscious insistence on the equal rights of husband and wife in marriage in 1 Corinthians 7:2-4. For Paul's reciprocal formulation of the prohibition of divorce, see below.

7. See, e.g., D. L. Dungan, *op. cit.*, pp. 102ff.

8. Except of course in the so-called "preteritive" interpretation, i.e., in the sense of an allusion to Deuteronomy 24:1 "notwithstanding"; this view has been most ably defended by Vawter, *art. cit.*, but few interpreters have found it a satisfactory explanation of the text. One would also have to except those interpretations which understand *porneia* to refer to concubinage, incestuous relationships and the like; see below.

9. The word for "divorce" is *aphienai*, not *apolyein* as in the Synoptics. It might be rendered "dismiss" or "put away," but the RSV (which we are citing here) is correct, since the sense is technical.

10. Literally, the brother or sister, i.e., the Christian partner, "is not enslaved," *ou dedoulōtai*. This is generally interpreted to mean that remarriage is allowed; see below.

11. See R. Bultmann, *The History of the Synoptic Tradition*, rev. ed. (New York: Harper & Row, 1968), pp. 132-136. We cannot of course repeat the details of such an analysis in this brief chapter.

12. Cf. Matthew's "ecclesiological" transformation of the confession of Peter at Caesarea Philippi (16:13-19) as well as of other Markan passages such as the storm on the lake (Mt 8:23-27); for the problem-solving concern of the Church, see also Matthew 18:15-20.

13. The principal exponent of this view was J. Bonsirven, *Le divorce dans le Nouveau Testament* (Tournai: Desclée, 1948).

14. It is true that *porneia* is not the ordinary word for adultery, as the very context shows. But it is quite possible that *porneia* was chosen precisely to generalize the concept of the unchastity that can break a marriage. In any case, Matthew does not use the language of Deuteronomy 24:1 (LXX). On this interpretation of the exceptive clauses, see among Catholic authors K. Haacker, "Ehescheidung und Wiederverheiratung im Neuen Testament," in *Theologische Quartalschrift* 151 (1971), pp. 28-38, and the survey of L. Sabourin, *art. cit.*, pp. 83-84.

15. Q. Quesnell has very ably argued, taking up a suggestion of J. Dupont, that the eunuch saying in Matthew 19:12 refers to those who accept the separation of a broken marriage without the right to remarry: " 'Made Themselves Eunuchs for the Kingdom of Heaven' (Mt 19, 12)," in *Catholic Biblical Quarterly* 30 (1968), pp. 335-358. But if this is correct, the real innovation in Jesus' teaching is the notion of separation without remarriage, and this seems only very obliquely stated in the various sayings of this pericope.

16. One must understand such a statement in the context of Matthew's presentation of the on-going validity of the law in the Jewish-Christian community even though Jesus has radicalized it; see the sayings in Matthew 5:17-20 and the essay of G. Barth in G. Bornkamm *et al.*, *Tradition and Interpretation in Matthew* (Philadelphia: Westminster Press, 1963).

17. Cf., e.g., W. J. O'Shea, "Marriage and Divorce: The Biblical Evidence," in *Australasian Catholic Record* 47 (1970), pp. 89-109; J. A. Grispino, *The Bible Now!* (Notre Dame: Fides, 1971), pp. 95-107.

18. One should compare carefully and objectively the antitheses in Matthew 5:21-48: "You, therefore, must be perfect, as your heavenly Father is perfect." In the immediate context of the divorce saying, the Church has long recognized idealistic hyperbole in the saying: "If your right hand causes you to sin, cut it off and throw it away," and Jesus' absolute prohibition of oaths has not only not been taken literally as law, but has been formally contravened even by ecclesiastical practice. It is difficult to refrain from exploiting this and other examples from Jesus' teaching when discussing the divorce statements. See J. A. Grispino, *op. cit.*, pp. 98-100 (references).

19. For discussion of the alternatives, see J. Jeremias, *The Sermon on the Mount* (Philadelphia: Fortress Press, 1963).

20. Cf., e.g., G. Schneider, "Jesu Wort über die Ehescheidung in der Überlieferung des Neuen Testaments," in *Trierer Theologische Zeitschrift* 80 (1971), pp. 65-87.

Bernard Häring, C.SS.R.

A Theological Appraisal of Marriage Tribunals

As a point of departure I would like to ask: How can we explain the fact that the Roman Catholic Church has developed so well the institution of marriage tribunals without equally developing the institution of marriage counselors? Was the main concern to heal marriages or to determine whether a dead marriage could be annulled? We have to see the whole problem against the background of a certain culture, a certain political organization, a particular theology, and especially a particular concept of validity of a sacramental contract. Also, how should the shift in the self-understanding of the Church from a chiefly institutional outlook to a more sacramental vision be reflected in the matter of marriage tribunals? These are some of the principal questions that theology can and must pose regarding the desirable reforms in this field.

The Legitimate Interest of the Church

Marriage is both institution and sacrament, and thus is a mirror-image of the Church which is, above all, the great sacrament of God's covenant with his people of his saving intention for all mankind, and must therefore be this also in the institutional aspects of her life. It is the sacramental reality of the Church that obliges her to give shape to her institutional reality; hence she is meant to be, in her whole life, a *visible* and incarnate sign of God's covenant fidelity and of his renewing and conciliating presence.

Facing the burning problem of the marriage tribunal and its structure and rationale, I want first of all to insist that the Church has a competence and important task in this field. But then the ecclesiology obliges us to ascertain whether there is a right proportion and harmony between the different tasks of the Church which is, above all, a sacrament of reconciliation and messenger of the Gospel and Gospel-morality, while juridical institutions must be subordinate to this essential character.

The prime mission of the Church regarding marriage is the proclamation of the good news that marriage is a graced sign of God's fidelity and mercy, a sign of God's gladdening and healing love. Juridical controls must hold a visibly subordinate place in comparison with the educative and reconciliatory role of the Church. The marriage catechumenate, the sexual education and the availability of well-prepared marriage counselors as truly competent "marriage doctors" are far more mandatory than the marriage tribunal whose actual role is to determine whether a thoroughly dead marriage can or cannot be declared to have been invalid from the very beginning.

One of the most intriguing aspects of our problem concerns the extent to which the Church can declare that, from the very beginning, certain types of marriages which are really meant to be lifetime covenants are non-valid. For instance, in today's mixed-marriage regulation, a marriage of two Protestants, one of whom happened to be baptized (but not educated) in the Catholic Church, is declared null and void unless he has received the Catholic dispensation from the canonical form of marriage contract. Such a marriage can become a very visible sign of love, fidelity and gracious forgiveness. What does it mean, then, to say that it is not valid? If one of the two spouses in such a marriage later becomes tired of his partner and falls in love with a Catholic who was never married or one who is also living in such an "invalid" marriage, these two are then considered free to marry each other canonically. Yet the new marriage, which by the standard of Canon Law and the marriage tribunal is declared to be a sacrament, can be a crying sign of injustice and infidelity. The spouse baptized in the Catholic Church may have divorced his partner in order to marry the other person, not for the Lord's sake and not according to his conscience which was formed by the biblical perspectives, but because he was seduced by lust.

This is only one extreme case of the possible "divorce" of the juridical aspect from the Gospel morality, but the very fact that these things were accepted uncritically by canonists and marriage tribunals is a cause of the crisis which now confronts us. However, we must not throw out the child with the bath water. The Church has a legitimate interest in the institutional aspect of marriage, although her first concern must be the moral and religious aspect. But the whole approach depends on how the relationship is seen between the institutional-juridical aspect and the reality of the sacrament as visible sign of grace.

Contract or Covenant?

The relationship between Yahweh and Israel, between Christ and his Church, is not to be called a contract but a covenant of love. Marriage is not a sacrament insofar as it is a contract but only insofar as it is a visible and graced image of the covenant between Christ and his Church. A marriage "contract" can be merely a sociological item which comes to the fore when, for instance, two clans or patriarchal (or matriarchal) families are stipulating a marriage. In this case the choice and the conditions of the contract are viewed mainly as for the benefit of clan—e.g., the family farm, the desired heirs, and so on. Even there, some covenant aspects exist, such as a guarantee of friendship through the marriage covenant, a real covenant between the two clans. One of the reasons for the polygamy of the kings and princes of Israel was that through their several wives they hoped to initiate or deepen the covenant with the different clans or neighboring tribes. But all this is not what we mean by sacrament-covenant; at least it cannot be the main perspective.

Marriage is a sacramental covenant if it reflects the great covenant, the union between Christ and his Church. But how can a naked contract between two interested families, even ratified by the two spouses, be called "sacrament" in a full sense if there is no mutual respect in love, trust and fidelity, if there is no real conjugal vow to love each other and to be faithful for better and for worse?

If the contract is the sacrament by its very judical nature and its juridical evidence, then it is relatively easy to control the validity of sacraments by marriage tribunals. If, however, the sacramental reality is the visibility of the gracious presence of Christ in the common striving of the spouses for ever greater love for each other, in the dedication to fidelity even to the point of redeeming the other from infidelity through generous forgiveness and reconciliation, and in the gracious "yes" to the mission of fatherhood and motherhood, then a very different picture emerges. The covenant aspect then comes to the foreground. The good of the persons, their capacity to love, the fostering of conditions that favor their growth in love, the experience of redemption and redeeming love, the readiness to forgive: all this will be the main interest of the Church.

But then—unfortunately—it will be much more difficult to determine the validity or non-validity of a marriage. Then also, the question of whether an existing marriage can be saved or not cannot so easily be ignored. How can we then so easily declare a marriage "invalid" which has all the signs of hope for working out as a covenant, and declare a marriage "valid" which no longer exists and cannot in any way be raised from death, and which from the very beginning gave little hope, from an anthropological point of view, that it could ever become a visible sign of the covenant between Christ and the Church?

The prevailing practice of marriage tribunals, in accordance with Canon Law and the approach of a certain moral theology, was radically marked by an absolute "tutiorism" which seemed to be an accepted system in all matters concerning a sacrament. As an approach in moral theology, the tutiorism tended always to decide for the formal structure of law and rules, with little concern and sensitivity for the needs of persons and the real opportunities to serve God. When the prevailing tutiorism in all sacramental questions joined the perspective which considered marriage chiefly as a contract, then an almost perfect control system for marriage tribunals was formed. When the juridically valid contract was automatically the "sacrament," then there was no need to ask whether a concrete marriage ever was meant as a visible sign of love, of concern, of mutual respect, fidelity and generous readiness for reconciliation. The absence of canonically invalidating impediments and the observance of the canonically valid form of the contract proved the validity of the *matrimonium ratum,* and the physical penetration of the vagina by the husband's penis was considered as sufficient proof of the consummation of the marriage (*matrimonium ratum et consummatum*). Therefore an official of the marriage tribunal did not need great knowledge of man and his life-conditions; with formalistic training in Canon Law he could easily exercise his control function.

Still, there was always in Canon Law at least one aspect which called for a more personalistic approach, namely, the determination of what was a valid consensus. Here is, therefore, an important point of departure. It only helps, however, if the whole context, theological and sociological, of the marriage tribunal is thoroughly taken into consideration and re-examined.

There is urgent need to study profoundly the anthropological conditions for an indissoluble marriage. Does a certain marriage, although it might fulfill the conditions for validity laid down by Canon Law, have any hopeful start toward becoming truly a sacramental reminder of Christ's presence and of the meaning of his covenant with the Church? The anthropological conditions will look different when we consider marriage more a covenant-sacrament than a contract-sacrament. If there is any place for tutiorism with respect to the sacraments, there must be much greater care to guarantee that the covenant-sacrament becomes a visible and effective sign of the one saving covenant between Christ and the Church. And no marriage should, then, be declared null and void if it bears in itself a genuine hope that it can work out as a salvific sign and event. Moreover, if marriage is truly a sacrament and covenant, it will affirm the calling to fruitfulness without degrading it to a bare means of procreation.

A concrete situation may explain better this matter of general considerations. Is a marriage with a totally disoriented homosexual husband consummated if he has intercourse with his wife while telling her, either in so many words or by his whole behavior, "It is not the real thing; I have pleasures only in intercourse with a male"? This intercourse might even have led to conception, but it is a most loveless and degrading experience that utterly contradicts the perspective of a covenant-sacrament characterized by mutual love and respect. On a human level this marriage seems to me not to be "consummated."

Juridical Control and Trust
in the Conscience of the Faithful

In order not to be misunderstood, I emphasize again that the Church has a legitimate interest in the sanctity of Christian marriage and a duty to watch over it and to exclude scandal. But the core question is: To what extent must the Church exercise her control in determined juridical forms?

The least we can say is that in an age of well-accepted paternalism and of a general lack of maturity among the laity, the system of controls has a far broader scope than in an age of general education and of a particular call to maturity in view of a pluralistic, dynamic society and Church. I think it does not imply an exaggerated apologetic approach if some of us assert that the structure of the marriage tribunal was fairly well adjusted to the possibilities and needs of a paternalistic age. But if this is true, the conclusion could be drawn that it is not at all adjusted to our present age and culture, where the emphasis must be much more on education toward maturity and toward trust in the upright conscience of the faithful. The Motu Proprio *Causas Matrimoniales* of Paul VI is an important step in the right direction. Nevertheless I think it is only a first step which forces us to continue the reflection and re-examination in dialogue with the critical generation of Christians of today and tomorrow.

Past practice has put almost all its trust in juridical controls and proofs. The witness of the persons directly involved has generally been considered as not reliable. An example, applicable to many other aspects, is the process about dispensation from an unconsummated marriage. Distasteful medical inspections about the existence of the "hymen virginale" were imposed even in cases of the most devout and exemplary Christians and even in cases where both partners agreed that the marriage had not been consummated.

The main question arises from the total context of today: Should not much more be left to the conscience of the persons? But to what extent? Perhaps a pluralism of practices according to the different cultures would be necessary here. There are parts of the Church where today the very fact that the partners are deeply interested in the recognition of the marriage by the official Church is sufficient sign that they are sincere and can and must be trusted. In a great many cases, those who want to conclude a new canonically valid marriage after the total failure of a first marriage have a well-informed conscience about the invalidity of the first marriage. They know with moral certainty that in the first marriage there was never, from its earliest moment, the slightest sign of hope for stability.

The theologian would most probably overstep the limits of his competence if he would dare to offer for the new situation concrete solutions in the form of juridical rules. However, I think that theologians, together with all those who are competent in the behavioral sciences, must call upon the Church authorities to take very seriously into consideration the profound transition from a paternalistic society, with its measure of control, to a culture which requires greater respect and trust in the upright conscience of the people. I am convinced that this re-examination would gradually lead to a totally new style of marriage tribunal.

A Reversal of the "Favor Juris"?

In the present legislation, and even more in the present practice of the marriage tribunals, there is an absolute *favor juris* (an absolute presumption of law) in favor of the validity of the previous marriage, even in cases where there is not the slightest hope to save or to rebuild it. A person whose first marriage has failed is obliged—under the gravest sanctions—to live a celibate life if there remains any juridical doubt in favor of the canonical validity of the dead marriage. Even in those cases where both the person with a well-informed conscience and the pastor are thoroughly convinced that the first marriage was never truly a marriage in the fully human and sacramental sense, this first marriage will always have the *favor juris*. The theological and juridical tutiorism wants to be absolutely sure that there will not be simultaneously two marriage contracts, both of which could perhaps have the character of contract-sacrament.

In this matter, too, besides the questionable theological and juridical tutiorism, we have to consider the sociological and cultural context. In the era during which the marriage tribunal took shape, the right of the human person to live in a marriage was not so strongly felt as it is today. Europe had reached a high degree of economic saturation; the number of family-farms and the little family enterprises could not be multiplied, and consequently many men and women could not get married. They either entered the "states of perfection," acquiring thus a higher social status, or they remained on the family-farm. Marriages did not normally fail externally because the whole social and economic order worked for stability of the institution. If, nevertheless, a marriage did fail, the persons re-entered the realm of the patriarchal family; they were not discriminated against or socially isolated. Now, the industrial revolution having made marriage possible for everyone who is able to build a family, the right to marry and to get married is among the most basic rights of the human person. If a marriage fails, however, the abandoned spouse cannot be reintegrated in a patriarchal family, since this type of family no longer exists. He or she therefore often remains an isolated being in the most pitiable human condition.

Is not this tremendous change in the world around us a sufficient reason to re-examine the approach of Canon Law with respect to the marriage tribunal? I would like to suggest that the *favor juris* be reversible. This would mean that while it is truly probable that the first marriage did not fulfill the anthropological, theological and canonical conditions for a valid sacramental marriage, it should still have the *favor juris* as long as there is a chance that it can be saved; but if it can no longer be saved—not even by the most generous action of reconciliation—the right of the person to marry and to get married should prevail against the doubtful validity of such a previous marriage. Nobody should, under the new social conditions, be obliged to lifelong celibacy on the mere ground of a slight probability that the previous marriage may have been valid. There should be no absolute tutiorism militating against the basic human right to marry.

Such a reversal would thoroughly change the structure of the marriage tribunals. Until now, the person whose first marriage failed has been always in the position of the accused person who has to bring a hundred percent proofs of the canonical invalidity of the destroyed marriage. If the *favor juris* were to be reversed, it would be the business of the marriage tribunal to prove that the person was validly married. The person could then state his or her case against the validity of the first marriage and would be free to follow his or her upright and well-informed conviction that the marriage never fulfilled the conditions of valid marriage. Unless the tribunal were able to prove the contrary, the person would not be deprived of one of the most basic human rights.

This reversal of the *favor juris,* according to which the right to marry and to get married would be "in possession," would call for a strong effort to form the conscience of the Christian and to be sincere before God and the Church. I insist that my proposal presupposes that, first of all, everything possible is to be done to save an existing marriage, including the most generous readiness to forgive and to be reconciled. It would refer only to those "marriages" which have never truly worked out and are thoroughly dead when the question is posed.

It is an open problem how, in the case of such reversal, this *favor juris* should be defined and what the degree of probability should be. Even now the present marriage tribunal is not meant to demand a metaphysical and absolute proof of the invalidity. A "moral certainty" should suffice. It needs a good deal of reflection and of formation of the mind of the marriage "judge" to see clearly what the expression "moral certainty" means; it is not always easy to define the degree of certainty for which he must aim. If my proposal—which is also made by many others—were accepted, then the question of probabilism becomes actual again: What degree of probability in favor of the invalidity of the first marriage is necessary for the application of the *favor juris* regarding the right to marry?

Possible Reintegration of the "Oikonomia" of the Orthodox Churches?

The proposed reversal of the *favor juris* would somehow remain within the mentality and tradition of the Occidental, Latin Church. It would still include the need for most serious reflection about the validity or non-validity of the previous marriage. Of course this reflection would also be based on the progressing insights into the nature of man and the covenant nature of a sacramental marriage.

The ecumenical climate invites us to face a further possible approach: that which we find throughout the whole history of the Oriental Churches, the "oikonomia."

I have not in mind to discuss here the whole approach of the Orthodox Churches; I shall limit myself to some hints. In the Oriental tradition there is no obsession with the question of validity of a contract-sacrament if a marriage is already thoroughly dead, since they have more in mind the covenant-sacrament. As a consequence, for them the Word of Christ, "What God has joined together man must not separate," forbids any separation, because a separation—as, e.g., Canons 1129 and 1130 foresee—means a real death of the marriage. The genuine Eastern tradition insists much more than our present Canon Law on the obligation of forgiveness and reconciliation. The ancient Oriental tradition does not favor any second marriage after the death of the spouse. Even beyond the physical death there remains something of the abiding sacramentality of this covenant experience for the whole lifetime of the widow or widower. But generally the prudence of the apostolic times was followed, suggesting rather a marriage than the danger to "burn" in wrongful desires or even in adultery (cf. 1 Tm 5:14).

If a marriage is hopelessly dead while the spouse is still alive, the Orthodox tradition does appeal to the abandoned spouse to choose celibacy for the heavenly kingdom: "Let those accept it who can" (Mt 19:12). However, faced with an abandoned spouse who, after all, does not feel able to live honestly and without great harm in a life of celibacy, the Orthodox tradition takes recourse in "oikonomia," which has a meaning similar to the virtue of "epikeia" in our best tradition. While there is no exception about the norm of saving a marriage as long as it can be saved, the Orthodox spirituality and practice allow exceptions after the total "death" of a marriage, in view of God's economy of salvation and in trust of God's mercy.

The final question is, then, not whether the previous marriage can be annulled, as in our tribunal approach. For them there are the following main questions: (1) Is it true that the first marriage cannot be saved or restored? (2) Is it true that this person cannot grasp the call to lifelong celibacy? (3) Would a new marriage have a chance to bring the person closer to salvation?

This kind of approach does not allow the same kind of marriage tribunals to develop as we saw in the Latin Church during the past centuries. It calls rather for "ministers of reconciliation," for an education toward celibacy wherever this may have a real chance to be understood, and for a pastoral council which is less concerned with the question of tutiorism with respect to the initial canonical validity of the dead marriage and more concerned for the future of the abandoned spouse and the good of the Church as a sacrament of both fidelity and mercy.

There is still hard and patient theological research needed before we dare to assert that the Roman Catholic Church could somehow adopt the outlook and practice of the Orthodox Churches, although we are inclined to suggest it, particularly in view of the situation of divorced, isolated persons in our modern society. It is clear that the principle of indissolubility of a sacramental marriage must not be denied or ignored. The Oriental tradition was convinced, however, that the application of "oikonomia," wherever the good of the person seems to request it strongly, does not deny the indissolubility but rather imposes simultaneously on the Church greater efforts to foster fidelity, reconciliation as long as there is hope, and stability of all marriages.

A partial and wise integration of the wisdom of the ancient Oriental tradition might help to transform the marriage tribunals into a more pastoral, pedagogical, constructive and forward-looking institution. Such a profound transformation might be better able to evidence the Church's competence and divine right to watch over the holiness of the Christian marriage.

John T. Noonan, Jr.

Ursa's Case

That law is not coextensive with a system of courts is often obscured by the dominance of the judicial model as the paradigm of law. Law is what a court decides; law without judicial enforcement is impalpable, a mere moral ideal—so law is frequently, but mistakenly considered. Law, however, exists whenever there is a social norm acknowledged by authoritative officials as controlling individual whim, wherever there are rules officially treated as governing similar situations. The judicial process, a particular means of establishing law, is distinguished from law in general by three distinct characteristics. It requires a dispute between two sides which must be judged. It requires a person distinct from the two sides to do the judging. It restricts the basis of judgment to testimony presented in a process in which both sides are heard. A law may exist without this special sort of proceeding to acknowledge or enforce it.

Once this simple and fundamental distinction is insisted upon, it is evident that for many centuries there was no judicial process in which a Christian could seek to terminate his marriage by divorce, annulment, or dispensation. Divorce, like marriage, was a form taken over by Christians from existing models. The two most relevant legal systems, the Jewish and the Roman, did not treat divorce as a judicial act. It was controlled by law and effected by the public but personal act of a party to the marriage contract. It dissolved marriage not through the decree of a court but through the decision of an individual spouse.

29

By the time of the composition of the Book of Deuteronomy, a procedure for lawful divorce was taken as established in Israel. If a man "found something shameful" in his wife, he was to make out a libel of repudiation, hand it to his spouse, and dismiss her from his house (Dt 24:1-4). Nothing was specified as to the husband proving something shameful, nothing as to the wife's judicially resisting the husband's unilateral determination. Only in the case where a man accused his wife of having been unchaste before marriage was provision made for a trial of his allegations (Dt 22:13-21). Here the penalty for the wife if the accusation were proved was death. Divorce as such was not viewed as a matter of justice.

Roman law was similarly structured. Divorce in classical Roman law consisted in the act of repudiation of the spouse. Post-classically, a written bill of divorce, *repudium*, was required. The action of a tribunal was not involved.[1]

With such procedures current, the New Testament itself and the Christian commentators upon it who discussed divorce made no reference to a judicial proceeding as the form in which divorce was granted. The writers who spoke only of the indissolubility of Christian marriage—Hermes, Athenagoras, Clement, Ambrose, Jerome, and Augustine—had no special need to consider the way in which divorce might be effective. The authors who permitted divorce for wifely adultery—Tertullian, Hilary, Ambrosiaster, Epiphanius, and Asterius—indicated that dissolution was effected by the husband.[2] Tertullian, for example, asks, "What will the husband among you do if his wife has committed adultery? Will he have her?" Unilaterally deciding that the *causa adulterii*, ground of adultery, is present, the husband lawfully dismisses, acting as the surrogate of God; the creator "disjoins what he himself has joined." Similarly, in Asia Minor, Bishop Asterius of Amasea declared that where adultery was committed by a wife, the husband rightfully divorced her. Licensed to do so by "the maker of all," the husband "breaks the bond." Origen speaks of Jesus divorcing his first bride, the synagogue, and marrying another; Jesus acts by giving a bill of divorce.[3]

Those who understood St. Paul's, "If the unbeliever leaves, let him leave" (1 Cor 7) to dissolve the marriage, understood the termination to occur without judicial action. Paul himself, as Daube has suggested, may have understood conversion itself as a coming into existence of a new man without marital ties, so that restoration of the old marriage depended entirely on the new man's new choice. In the interpretation put forward in fourth-century Rome, the unbeliever's action in withdrawing was decisive: "Contempt of the creator dissolves the law of marriage." The phrase was legal; its author, like Tertullian, was probably a lawyer; but no judicial process was envisaged. In whatever way Paul's exception to indissolubility was explained, dissolution did not depend upon a court.[4]

Ecclesial exercise of power over the dissolution of marriage of believers was not, however, unknown. The New Testament itself offered the instance of Paul's pronouncement on the man who had taken his father's wife. Physically absent from Corinth, but present in spirit, Paul delivered the man's body up to Satan that his spirit might be saved. In Paul's own words he had "judged him in the name of the Lord Jesus" (1 Cor 5:4-5). Implicit in this verdict was the annulment of the man's union with his stepmother, described by Paul as *porneia*, sheer sexual impurity. But Paul, following the rabbinic precedents with which he was familiar, did not appear to think that a judgment of this kind required any hearing for the man and his chosen wife. The facts were notorious. No judicial form seemed necessary for judgment to be passed upon them.

Later episcopal action in the pre-Constantinian era seems marked by the same pastoral freedom from form. According to Origen, "some leaders of the Church" permitted divorced women to remarry during the lives of their husbands. They did so "outside of Scripture," but they did not act "wholly unreasonably." They showed "indulgence" in order to avoid worse, permitting what was "beyond what was intended and written from the beginning." Their attitude, said Origen, was comparable to St. Paul's conceding remarriage to widows. Origen did not suggest that the bishops had examined or could examine the validity of the women's first marriages or the justice of their divorces. Freedom to remarry appeared here to depend on the wise exercise of administrative authority, not upon a judicial decision.[5]

Precedent, nonetheless, existed for the judicial control of divorce. It was to be found in those systems, Jewish and Roman, which did not make divorce itself a judicial act. The analogies which they afforded were ultimately irresistible.

Rabbinic Judaism had elaborated procedural rules for the validity of a libel of repudiation. It had to be properly signed, dated, and witnessed. It had to be properly written not in juice, but in any lasting substance, on any durable material including the horn of an ox or the hand of a slave. It had to be properly delivered to the woman herself; to put it in her lap or her work-basket, for example, sufficed, but not to throw it on the floor from the bed. It had to be specially authenticated when delivered to a wife in a different country. It had to take effect before the husband's death. It could be conditioned on the payment of money by the wife. These technical conclusions, filling one substantial volume of the Talmud, point to considerable social supervision of the process of divorce. As Falk contends, their development from the first century on made it likely that a divorcing spouse would have the libel of divorce made out by an official scribe, so that no mistake would be made. Non-literate persons would have depended on the scribe in any event. Litigation concerning the validity of the *Get* could be carried on before a *Beth-din* or court composed of three Jews learned in the law. Although not decreeing divorce themselves, such courts brought divorce within the judicial realm.[6]

Beyond procedural correctness, a *Beth-din* could give judgment in areas proximate to divorce. It could authorize a woman to remarry after she had presented proof that her absent husband was dead. It could determine that a woman had violated one of the commandments—in this case, if she were divorced she lost the dowry which otherwise returned to her upon dissolution of the marriage. The Babylonian Talmud preserves the record of an elaborate plot by which a husband anxious to divorce but to keep the dowry sought to convict his wife of participation in an orgy; the *Beth-din* detected his fraudulent use of egg yolk to simulate semen and punished the crime. A Jewish law court could also compel a husband to issue a *Get* if he were denying his wife conjugal support. Exercising such a power, the court was separated from a tribunal granting a divorce only by a fiction. In each of these types of substantive decision-making divorce became a matter of justice.[7]

Finally, the existence or non-existence of a marriage must at least occasionally have been pronounced upon when illegitimacy was at issue. Biblical law was extraordinarily harsh in the consequences prescribed for a person born of a union within the prohibited degrees of consanguinity and affinity. "No child of an incestuous union may be admitted into the congregation of the Lord, nor any descendant of his even to the tenth generation" (Dt 23:3). The bastard was a *mamzer,* excluded from the community of Israel by virtue of the holiness of the community, and the bastard's children were, like their father or mother, stained by the sin of their ancestors. Talmudic law expanded the ban to any offspring of an Israelite and a slave, an Israelite and a heathen, or an Israelite and a married woman. With the rule claiming a hold on "ten generations," genealogical records were maintained to distinguish the legitimate from the illegitimate. If a court were also asked to make the distinction, as it surely must have been, it necessarily decided whether a marriage stood at the beginning of the line or not.[8]

Jewish procedure still stopped short of making the validity of a divorce turn on a judicial decision. When Shammai said that "the something shameful" in Deuteronomy referred to serious moral fault and Hillel said it could mean a matter as idiosyncratic as cooking unpleasing to the husband, the opinion of Shammai was not likely to win out unless a court was ready to measure the quantum of fault. Conversely, as Hillel's views prevailed, litigation was not invited as to the ground for divorce. The Jewish practice related the termination of marriage to a judicial system without making termination normally dependent on a court.[9]

Roman law, under Christian influence, made a closer connection. Constantine specified a limited number of grounds on which divorce might be justified. The act of repudiation remained the act of divorce, but failure to have observed the grounds was punishable—in the case of a wife by forfeiture of her property and deportation to an island, in the case of a husband by loss of his wife's dowry and the denial of his right to remarry.[10] Enforcement of such penalties depended on a disappointed spouse taking action through the courts, but if he or she chose to sue, a court would have the opportunity to determine the justice of the divorce.

The creation of a forum in which divorce must be justified went back to the echo of Shammai and Hillel in Matthew: "Is it lawful for any cause (aitia) for a man to put away his wife?" (Mt 19:3). Those Christians who found a cause sanctioned by the answer of the Lord excepting sexual immorality (porneia) saw divorce as a requirement of justice. For them a tribunal of justice—so that a man should not decide his own case—was a logical, if unacknowledged necessity. The grounds for divorce admitted by the Christian emperors were larger than porneia in a strict sense, but not more liberal than a broad reading of porneia might allow. Although some leading Christians believed that any exception to indissolubility was wrong, the emperors probably legislated with a sense of following one school of acceptable opinion on a debated issue. Epiphanius, for example, spoke of divorce for porneia or for adultery or for other cause—what was vital for him was the cause (aitia), not the technical meaning of the Lord's word porneia. To give a forum to a spouse unjustly dismissed on a ground not specified by law was a practical response to one reading of the Gospel. "The justice of divorce," wrote Tertullian, "has Christ as its defender." [11]

Suppose, however, that both parties to a union desired its dissolution. The principle that marriage could be dissolved by mutual consent was ingrained in classical Roman law and untouched by the Christian emperors until 449, when Theodosius II prohibited the practice. Even then no teeth were put into the prohibition. The courts were no help if the consent was truly mutual, and the Church had no machinery which could enforce the imperial rule by external sanctions. Only in 542, in Justinian's second extensive effort at divorce reform, was consensual divorce threatened with effective secular punishment. If a woman divorced without legal cause, two-thirds of her property was to go to her children, one-third to a monastery, and the bishop of the city of her domicile was to enclose her in a monastery for life. In 548 the same penalties were extended to a man divorcing without cause. Responsibility for enforcement was assigned to the bishops.[12]

Secular prohibitions of consensual divorce lasted no more than a decade, being abrogated by Justinian's successor upon the complaint of many couples.[13] What the brief but strenuous effort at suppression did suggest was that only the Church would have the interest and the institutions to act against consensual divorce. It also suggested the ineffectiveness of a judicial handling of the matter. The penalties themselves had been designed medicinally, cancelable in toto, according to Justinian's final legislation in 556, if the guilty decided to live together after all.[14] Yet such medicine was too strong for the machinery of the law to administer; and it may not unreasonably be supposed that the burden on the bishops to investigate, accuse, try and judge the offense of consensual divorce taxed their resources beyond their capabilities.

Involvement of the bishops with the policing of consensual divorce—a dubious exercise of judicial power, for could the bishop be accuser and judge both?—had much earlier been preceded by the bishops' involvement with true judicial decision-making as to marriage. That bishops should be judges was a foregone conclusion when Paul did not take literally the Lord's "Judge not lest you be judged" (Mt 7:1) and urged the converts of Corinth to submit their disputes to Christian judges (1 Cor 6:4). That Paul's own advice to choose as judges "those who are rated as nothing in the

Church" should also not be taken literally was also a foregone conclusion if the judgments were to have binding force in an expanding community. Hence the bishops had for many years been judges when Constantine, in one of his first public favors to Christianity, decreed that recourse to "episcopal judgment" should be recognized by the state.[15]

Marriage cases must have been among those matters brought to be tried, as Constantine said, "by the Christian law." But no evidence survives from the fourth century.[16] The first documented case is that of Ursa against Fortunius, decided by Innocent I in the wake of Alaric's invasion of 409 and reported by the pope himself as follows:

The turbulence of the barbarian hurricane has brought a case within the power of the laws. For, to a well-established marriage between Fortunius and Ursa, the onset of captivity had brought a blemish, unless the sacred statutes of religion were providing otherwise. When the said woman Ursa was held in captivity, the aforesaid Fortunius is known to have entered another marriage with Restituta. But, returned by the favor of the Lord, Ursa approached Us, and, with no one denying it, established that she was the wife of the aforesaid man. Therefore, Sir—deservedly illustrious son—We have decreed, with the approval of the Catholic faith, that that is the marriage which was first founded with divine grace; and the union of the second woman, while the first lives and has not been expelled by divorce, cannot by any means be legitimate.[17]

Probus, Innocent's correspondent, was presumably a Roman official—the "Sir" and the "illustrious" indicate official status. He was also a Christian—the Roman bishop's "son"; and Innocent has judged it appropriate to remind him of this relation. Highly legal in flavor, with "saids" and "aforesaids" and "decrees," this document appears to be a certificate to the civil official who would have responsibility for making the bishop's order effective.

Opportunity for the defendant to have been heard seems to be implicit in the formal phrase "no one denying it." Nothing, however, is said to indicate that Restituta had had her day in court to defend her marriage. Her union with Fortunius is annulled on the ground of *ligamen* without it being thought necessary to hear her argument; or perhaps notice to Fortunius was taken as sufficient. There is still something of an inquiry ex officio about the case, but on the whole it appears as a judgment issued after hearing.

Does the phrase "not expelled by divorce" imply that a different result would have followed if Fortunius, instead of relying on Ursa's enslavement, had formally divorced her? What is intended is probably an additional argument against Fortunius—he had not alleged any basis for lawful divorce; the implication that Innocent would have acted differently if he had shown cause for divorce goes beyond a proper reading of the document.

Authority for Innocent's certificate to Probus had one of two possible bases. In 399 the Emperor Honorius had specifically restricted episcopal judgments to matters *de religione,* "concerning religion"; other causes were to be heard "by the laws." By decree in 408, the emperor had ordered that public officials execute episcopal judgment in cases where the parties had agreed to the bishops' jurisdiction. Was Ursa's case one where Fortunius had agreed to the bishop's court, or was Innocent invoking the decree of 399 with an implication that public power should enforce a decision concerning religion? Although it seems to be implied that Fortunius was a Catholic, who could have been under threat of excommunication to agree to the bishop's court, Innocent says that the case has fallen within "the power of the laws." The decree of 399 must be meant. The bishop is judging a matter *de religione.*[18]

Innocent has further need to establish the religious character of his judgment. According to civil law, enslavement terminated a marriage, just as death did, and no further legal action was necessary to dissolve the union. Captivity was the same as slavery. By Roman law, Fortunius was no longer bound to Ursa after her capture; he had acted within his rights in remarrying. Hence, as Innocent notes, the first marriage would have had a blemish if the Catholic faith were not to provide otherwise. The religious law is being applied in derogation of the civil law.[19]

Scripture itself is not cited in the judgment. But "founded with divine grace" is a curial circumlocution for "what God has joined together." "Blemish" (*naevum*) recalls the language of Ephesians 5:27-28: Christ delivered himself up in order to present the Church "without blemish. Even thus ought husbands also to love their wives as their own bodies." The patterning of human marriages on the union of Christ and the Church is insinuated.

From Ursa's point of view the episcopal action was not an annulment at all, but the vindication of an existing marriage. That a court of the Church would be more sympathetic to her plea than a merely civil court made it understandable that she would invoke the episcopal authority—all the stronger in this instance because the bishop was the bishop of Rome. For the pope, his action upheld a marriage and proclaimed the faith; the annulment was incidental to his giving judgment.[20]

Desire on the part of deserted spouses like Ursa to have their rights declared and desire on the part of ecclesiastical authority to protect the Catholic doctrine on marriage had worked together to produce a forum in which true judicial power to uphold or to annul a marriage was exercised. The justice of annulment had the pope as its defender. A long march, unended over three quincentenaries later, was underway.

NOTES

1. *Digesta Iustiniani* 24.1.64 (classical law); *Codex Iustiniani* 5.17.8 (post-classical law). For a detailed study see Ernst Levy, *Hergang der römischen Ehescheidung* (Weimar: Hermann Böhlaus Nachfolger, 1925), pp. 86-95, 104.

2. Hilary, *Commentarium in evangelium Matthaei 22, Patrologia latina*, ed. J. P. Migne, vol. 9, col. 939; Ambrosiaster, *Commentarium in primam epistolam B. Pauli ad Corinthios, Patrologia latina*, vol. 17, col. 208; Epiphanius, *Panarion* 2.1.59, *Patrologia graeca*, vol. 41, cols. 1024-1025. For Tertullian and Asterius, see *infra*, n.3.

3. Tertullian, *Adversus Marcionem* 4.34, *Patrologia latina* 2.442; Asterius, *Homilia 5 in evangelium Matthaei, Patrologia graeca* 40.236; Origen, *Commentarium in evangelium Matthaei, Patrologia graeca* 14. 1244.

4. David Daube, "Pauline Contributions to a Pluralistic Culture: Re-Creation and Beyond," in *Jesus and Man's Hope*, ed. Donald G. Miller and Dikran Y. Hadidian (Pittsburgh: University of Pittsburgh Press, 1971), pp. 232-239; Ambrosiaster, *Commentarium in primam epistulam B. Pauli ad Corinthios* 7.13, *Patrologia latina* 17.219.

5. Origen, *Commentarium in evangelium Matthaei, Patrologia graeca* 14.1244-1245.

6. Mishnah 2a and 18b, Gemara 2a, *Gitten, The Babylonian Talmud,* trans. and ed. I. Epstein (London: The Soncino Press 1936) (on the requirements as to signature, dating, witnesses, materials, and authentication of a *Get*); Mishnah 77a and Gemara 77a, *Gittin* (on delivery); Mishnah 74a, *Gittin* (on *Get* conditioned on payment); Ze'ev Falk, *Jewish Matrimonial Law in the Middle Ages* (Oxford: at the Clarendon Press, 1966), p. 122 (on the probable effect of the technical requirements channeling divorce to the scribes). On the development of biblical law, see Reuven Yaron, "On Divorce in Old Testament Times," in *Revue internationale des droits de l'Antiquité* (1957), pp. 117-128.

7. Mishnah 87b, *Yebamoth, The Babylonian Talmud,* ed. Epstein (on authorization of remarriage after husband's death); Gemara 57a, *Gittin* (on the fraudulent effort to bilk a wife of her dowry); Gemara 63a, *Kethuboth, The Babylonian Talmud* (on compulsory *Get*).

8. Mishnah 49a, *Yebamoth* (on who are bastards); Gemara 49b, *ibid.* (on the genealogies of bastards).

9. Mishnah 90a, *Gittin* (Shammai and Hillel).

10. *Codex Theodosianus* 3.16.1.

11. Epiphanius, *Panarion* 2.1.59, *Patrologia graeca* 41.1024-1025. (This interpretation of Epiphanius reads him as referring to the termination of marriage by divorce as well as by death.) Tertullian, *Adversus Marcionem* 4.34, *Patrologia latina* 2.442. For another example of how broadly the Lord's exception in Matthew could be understood, see Augustine who argues that the cause necessary for separation, not termination of a marriage, is "fornicatio" but that "we are compelled to understand 'fornication' as a general universal term," standing for any desire "which makes the soul stray from the law of God by a bad use of the body" (*De sermone Domini in monte,* 1.16.46, *Corpus scriptorum ecclesiasticorum latinorum*). For further argument on the division of opinions among Christians being reflected in imperial divorce legislation, see John T. Noonan, Jr., "Novel 22," in *The Bond of Marriage,* ed. William W. Bassett (Notre Dame: The University of Notre Dame Press, 1968), pp. 71-90.

12. *Codex Iustiniani* 5.17.8 (Theodosius II); *Novel* 117.10 (Justinian, 542); *Novel* 127.4 (Justinian, 548). It has been plausibly argued that Theodosius II should not be read as prohibiting divorce by consent and that the first actual prohibition is Justinian's: Reuven Yaron, "De Divortio Varia," in *Revue d'histoire du droit* 32 (1964), p. 552.

13. *Novel* 140.

14. *Novel* 134.11.3.

15. *Codex Theodosianus* 1.27.1. Although the authenticity of this decree of 318 has been challenged, it and a related decree of 333 are probably authentic: Jean Gaudemet, *L'église dans l'empire romain* (Paris: Sirey, 1959), pp. 231-233.

16. Gaudemet, *op. cit.*, p. 234.

17. Innocent I, *Epistola* 36, *Patrologia latina* 20.602-603. *Regesta Pontificum Romanorum*, ed. P. Jaffé (Leipzig, 1885), p. 313. The text, edited by Pierre Coustant, read as follows: "Conturbatio procellae barbaricae facultati legum intulit casum. Nam bene constituto matrimonio inter Fortunium et Ursam captivitatis incursus fecerat naevum, nisi sancta religionis statuta providerent. Cum enim in captivitate praedicta Ursa mulier teneretur aliud conjugium cum Restituta Fortunius memoratus inisse cognoscitur. Sed favore Domini reversa Ursa nos adiit et nullo diffitente, uxorem se memorati perdocuit. Quare, domine fili merito illustris, statuimus, fide catholica suffragante, illud esse conjugium, quod erat primitus gratia divina fundatum; conventumque secundae mulieris, priore superstite, nec divortio ejecta, nullo pacto posse esse legitimum."

18. *Codex Theodosianus* 16.11.1 (decree restricting bishops to causes *de religione*); *ibid.*, 1.27.2 (decree ordering officials to execute episcopal judgment in cases where parties had agreed to jurisdiction). Gaudemet, *op. cit.*, p. 240, offers two fifth-century instances of excommunication threatened for avoidance of the episcopal tribunal. Ambrose had vigorously asserted to the Emperor Valentinian the exclusive competence of bishops in *causa fidei vel ecclesiastica: Epistola, Patrologia latina* 16.1003.

19. *Digesta Iustiniani* 23.2.1; 49.15.14 (on slavery ending marriage).

20. Judgments of the bishops of Rome were not able to be appealed: Zosimus, *Epistola* 12, *Patrologia latina* 20.676. *Regesta Pontificum Romanorum*, ed. P. Jaffé (Leipzig, 1885), p. 342.

Vernon J. Bourke

Marital Fidelity and Philosophy

A philosophical consideration of the bond of marriage should differ from a legal or a theological approach. If one views matrimony as an institution stemming from some sort of law (eternal, ecclesiastical, civil, or whatever), discussion must be in terms of what such law, or its maker, requires and prohibits. There is always something "positive" about such a legal approach, in the sense that given a certain set of commands the character of the institution is determined by these ordinances. To ask whether the laws are justified is an attempt to go beyond the laws to something more ultimate—either to a higher law or to some other principle of rectification. Similarly, in a theological context, marriage may be seen in terms of a set of religious beliefs that have been developed by critical examination into a more or less coherent and conscious systematization.[1]

Philosophy, as I understand it, implies some over-all natural reflection on reality, man and his experiences. It is not a science in the modern sense but an attempt at gaining ultimate wisdom. However, there is today no single, universally accepted philosophy; nor is there one philosophical point of view on marriage. In what follows, I shall attempt to speak of the several philosophical positions that are of contemporary relevance, but my own preference is for an epistemological realism with roots in the classic tradition of philosophy. In spite of the eclipse that has come over Thomistic philosophy after Vatican II, I am still convinced of the general validity of the philosophy that is implicit in the writings of Aquinas. This is not to say that my mind is closed to all that is being done in recent philosophies.

What really is the character of marriage as a philosopher might understand it? First of all, he does not know matrimony as a sacrament; or, if he is aware of its sacramental character in a certain religious context, he also knows that marriage is practiced in many cultures and celebrated in sections of the Christian world as something other than a sacrament.[2]

In point of fact, philosophers have variously regarded marriage as a human partnership, as a politico-social institution, as a career, and as a special mode of life. More recent thinkers take it to be a union of minds, a metaphysical bonding of a couple into a unified being, an essay in inter-subjectivity, or a meeting in love.[3]

One way of attempting to understand marriage is to compare it with human sexuality. They overlap, I think, but are not co-extensive. Sexuality is something that humans are born with: it is a natural characteristic which makes procreation possible and it modifies the psychic attitudes of man as well as his physical organism. Sexuality does not require marriage for its existence or functioning, but throughout the recorded history of mankind some type of marital society has been thought necessary or advisable for the proper exercise of sexuality. Marriage, on the other hand, is a kind of interpersonal association which need not be entered into by all humans. It involves some sort of special agreement between spouses to live and work together for a distinctive purpose. Conjugal society must have a definite goal that distinguishes it from business partnerships and bridge teams.

It seems quite clear to me that this objective for which the *institution* of marriage continues to exist, through the centuries, is to provide for the generating and upbringing of children. If children could be produced and well cared for in some other institution, marriage would not survive as a social institution. It is quite wrong, I think, to claim that some other end, such as mutual personal fulfillment, is the primary reason for conjugal society.[4] The *finis operis* of marriage is centered on progeny. Not all marriages achieve this objective, nor is it necessary that they do. Spouses need not have this end primarily in mind when they marry. All that is necessary is that their purposes in marrying not be in opposition to the reason why marriage was instituted.

Obviously some people marry who know that they cannot produce children. Their ends (as individual agents) may embrace mutual love, personal assistance, the avoidance of loneliness and many such goals. There is no immorality in marrying, under such conditions, for the sake of these secondary benefits. But all should recognize that these ends are derivative. We would not need marriage if children did not enter the picture.

This is not a view peculiar to a Catholic philosopher. Most people look on marriage as a means of setting up a home with the prospect of having children. Young people see it this way today. As one expert observer of today's youth puts it:

Post-modern youth are non-ascetic, expressive, and sexually free. . . . Marriage is increasingly seen as an institution for having children, but sexual relationships are viewed as the natural concomitant of close relationships between the sexes.[5]

Complete and most satisfactory fulfillment of sexual instincts can only be accomplished in marriage; it is the best available means of protecting the interests of both male and female spouses, and of their children. E. O. James (professor of the history and philosophy of religion at the University of London) has expressed this very well:

The ultimate purpose of the [sexual] union for which it was primarily devised biologically unquestionably is the perpetuation of the species, but man is so organized that he is more than a biological organism. He is capable of mutual love between the sexes and requires this quality in the environment of a home and family for the nurture and well-being of his offspring. Therefore the institution of marriage is an essential requirement to fulfill these three conditions, propagation, marital love and the upbringing of the young in the right *milieu* of a home.[6]

In fact we can conclude that both human sexuality and the social institution of marriage are functionally directed to the production of children, but the monogamous family provides for the nurture of offspring, while the simple exercise of sexuality does not. The psychologist J. A. Hadfield states the situation quite well: "The chief end of nature is the reproduction of the species and perpetuation of a healthy race." So he concludes, "For the establishment and maintenance of family life monogamous instincts were developed." [7]

Contemporary Philosophies on Marital Fidelity

Phenomenology is one of the most influential types of recent philosophy, particularly in continental Europe. We will take it as inclusive of existentialism, since most existentialists use the phenomenological method, and few professional philosophers now call themselves existentialists. Like Descartes, phenomenologists begin with a close examination of the presentations of personal consciousness. They endeavor to find what is essential, of ultimate significance, in these mental appearances. Since this starting point is subjective, even though there is a good deal of talk about "objects" and intentionality, there remains an aura of idealism about most versions of phenomenology. When the phenomenologist talks about the "world," it seems to be a projection from his own conscious experiences that he intends and not an independent cosmos. This is why little is done, or can be done, in the philosophy of science by phenomenologists.

Almost all phenomenological writings, on the other hand, have some moral coloration. There are few formal treatises on ethics, but one of the main concerns of this kind of philosophy is with the ethical problem: How may a person live well?

Generally, phenomenologists maintain that personal freedom is the greatest moral value. The great moral question, as they see it, centers on how to maximize one's own freedom without diminishing the freedom of other persons. So exalted is this notion of liberty within consciousness that anything which appears to restrain it is downgraded. Thus laws of any kind are not acceptable, since rules of behavior (from the divine to the lowest municipal ordinance) are taken as restrictions on personal freedom. The "authentic" man is antinomian. Hence there can be no existentialist philosophy of law.

Nor is much to be found in phenomenological literature on matrimony. One would not look to Jean-Paul Sartre and Simone de Beauvoir for marriage counseling. However, there is a great deal of emphasis on the importance of the person, on the role of intersubjectivity, on the relation of one person to another. The "I-Thou" relation is one of the chief themes in phenomenological writings.

Jean Nabert, for instance, has written beautifully about the importance of interpersonal communication. All growth in conscious personality depends on intercommunication with another.[8] As applied to the married relationship, this would mean that for their own good husband and wife should treat each other as persons and never as mere objects. To this important theme we will return.

Of course, there are many variations of viewpoint among phenomenologists: some are atheists; others have deep religious convictions. Paul Ricoeur and Jean Nabert are examples of Protestant thinkers in this school; Martin Buber was Jewish, Gabriel Marcel is Catholic. In the case of Marcel, we have a book that is important to our subject. In French it was entitled *Du refus à l'invocation* (1940), but the English title, *Creative Fidelity*, puts a happy emphasis on its pertinence to our present interest.[9] Marcel sees the conjugal relation as "the closest and perhaps the most fundamental of all personal relationships." [10] He distinguishes between a low-grade meaning of marital fidelity in which spouses maintain their marriage (often for the sake of children) because it is their duty, and that higher union of husband and wife as persons who are mutually "present" to each other.[11] Even in the marriage that has lost mutual love as its bond, however, there may be a still higher basis for permanence. This would be the foundation of the conjugal union as a sacrament, the fact that it is "rooted in God." [12] One wonders how much of this thinking is really philosophical and how much Marcel owes to his undoubted Christian convictions.

In the early pages of *Creative Fidelity* Marcel tries very hard to grasp the essence of the body-soul problem in man. This is important, since traditional Catholic thinking on marriage is often accused of putting too much emphasis on the bodily, objective and biological aspects of conjugal union. Marcel denies that the body-soul relation can be defined objectively. It is not a causal relation or a psycho-physical parallelism. He insists that he is his body but that he is not identical with his body.[13] But later he seems to reduce his existence to an act of self-affirmation: "If *to be* means *to affirm oneself, I am.*" [14] This does preserve the unity of the human person but at the cost of granting little reality to the corporeal side of man. After all, if human agents were angels we would not have to worry about marriage.

So, what is most distinctive in phenomenology as an approach to the conjugal relation is its strong emphasis on the person and on conscious freedom as constitutive of personhood.

Analytic philosophy is most prominent in English-speaking countries today. It has an abundant ethical literature, mostly in the field of the logic of ethical discourse, or meta-ethics.[15] Applied ethics is not so much cultivated and it is not easy to find an analytic study of marriage. However, the philosophy of law is quite important, particularly in the writings of H. L. A. Hart. On the whole, the moral aspects of sexual behavior are regarded as outside the domain of law. Any attempt to treat marital problems in terms of either state or Church law would be rejected by the typical analytic philosopher.

Much discussed by analysts, however, is the morality of

promise-keeping. Ever since Immanuel Kant's use of the lying promise to illustrate the categorical imperative, this has been a favorite theme in modern ethics. How is it that a person who makes a promise may be considered to place an obligation on himself? To what extent may self-imposed duties be morally binding? Does it make sense to speak of imposing an *absolute* obligation on oneself? [16] Usually the analytic philosopher will grant only a limited and relative degree of obligation to self-imposed commitments.[17] This would mean that, *in most cases,* a self-imposed promise is ethically binding, but the analyst sees the practical possibility of exceptional circumstances which could void any promise. Legal efforts to make people keep their promises (in married life or elsewhere) would, then, find little support in analytic philosophy.

John Wilson is a good example of a British analyst who does have something to say on conjugal fidelity.[18] He speaks rather forcefully in favor of the argument that parents have an obligation to keep their wedding promises until death, in view of the need of children to continued care and support, on the part of both parents. Thus he quotes with approval the statement that "the permanency of marriage is thus revealed as a biological fact, as a result of maturation and proof of achieved maturity." [19] This would not mean, of course, that Wilson totally disapproves of divorce for the childless couple who are in marital trouble, or indeed for all parents with dependent children.

Probably the outstanding feature of analytic ethics in reference to marital fidelity is the strong insistence that one cannot find ethical justification for the enforcement by law of private moral views. As Lord Devlin said at the beginning of a noted lecture on the subject:

There are still many Christians who regard marriage as absolutely indissoluble, and it is very possible that as a matter of Christian doctrine they are right. But if they were to seek to have that idea embodied in the law of the land, they would have to rely on doctrine and not upon morals. It is no longer generally thought in this country [England] to be morally wrong that a marriage should be dissolved and the spouses free to marry again.[20]

Humanism is today the name of a broad set of views on ultimate questions, rather than a particular school of philosophy. Existentialists, naturalists, analysts, Freudians, and many other types of thinkers may call themselves humanists. What distinguishes this sort of humanism is the blunt rejection of personal immortality, the existence of God, institutional religion. The humanist usually looks to "science" (or scientific method) as an ultimate discipline.[21] Freedom is almost an absolute value for most humanists, but, unlike phenomenologists who center freedom in subjective consciousness, the humanist thinks of liberty as the absence of external restraints.[22]

As a consequence the humanist judges the institution of marriage in relation to the public welfare. He is inclined to avoid absolute judgments and laws. Thus H. J. Blackham (ex-chairman of the British Humanist Association) writes:

Rules of a democratic society of all kinds, from rules of the road to rules of the courts, from statutes to contracts and promises, imply good faith and public spirit. They are not to be thought of as commandments or taboos, but rather as instruments of co-existence and cooperation in a free society for the sake of self-realization for all.[23]

Such a philosophical stance implies a rejection of the sanctioning of marital fidelity by a legal bond. For the humanist, spouses remain married as long as they respect each other's dignity and personal freedom, and especially as long as their marriage contributes to the good of organized society. Religion should have nothing to say about marital problems.[24]

Personalism (like humanism) is a generic philosophical attitude rather than a specific school of thought. The typical personalist has some idealistic antecedents: he thinks that the mind is more real and important than the body. He frequently associates his philosophic thinking with religious beliefs.

There are Christian personalists of many varieties. Unlike the "Christian ethicist" however (who tends to find his moral standards in Scripture and Reformed Church traditions), the personalist is a philosopher who is willing to offer rational or empirical grounds for his views.

One of the most effective writers on marriage, from this point of view, is P. A. Bertocci. His writings are well known and frequently cited by Catholic scholars.[25] Bertocci sees divorce as a personal and social catastrophe. His tendency is to stress the positive marriage ideals: mutual trust, respect and high-minded love. A good deal of support for the permanency of marriage is thus to be found in personalist writings. How much of this is truly philosophical and how much an idealist inheritance from Christian backgrounds is hard to determine.

Marxist philosophy should not be ignored on the contemporary scene. In Europe two kinds of ethical absolutism are recognized today: Catholic Scholasticism and theoretical Marxism.[26] Probably neither is as dogmatic as critics suggest, but the moral views of the Marxist philosopher may be at least as influential in the present world as are those of any major school of thought.

While its orientation is socio-political, theoretical Marxism also presents itself as a humanism. That is to say, the Marxist philosopher thinks that man is the most important being in existence. He also thinks that man is much more than a cog in the machine of industry. The ideal Marxist man is supposed to be well informed, honest, free to form his own moral judgments, and devoted to the welfare of all humanity.[27] Since 1950 there has been a remarkable growth of interest in ethics among Marxist thinkers, above all in Russia.

The attitude toward divorce in the U.S.S.R. has undergone decided changes in this century. Immediately after the revolution of 1917, divorce was granted by Soviet courts practically on demand. In the 1940's this permissive attitude ended. The Supreme Court of the U.S.S.R. then ruled that divorce could only be granted where "continuation of the marriage would conflict with the principles of communist morals and could not create the conditions necessary to family law and the rearing of children." [28] Family law is a separate division of legal practice in the Soviet Union.

In 1961 the *Moral Code of the Builder of Communism* was issued in Moscow. Point Eight enjoined "mutual respect in the family, and concern for the upbringing of children." [29] Promiscuity and adultery are indirectly disapproved in Point Seven. As De George points out, recent thinking in Russia has been entirely on the side of strengthening the family relationship and insisting on the obligation to raise children in the spirit of communist morality which is not without some puritanical elements.[30]

Oddly then, present-day Marxist philosophy supports the idea that marriage should be monogamous and lasting. The reasons for such a position may be largely a matter of party propaganda, but the fact of the matter is that Catholics are far from being the only people in the world who frown on divorce *a vinculo*.

Somewhat the same view obtains in some of the literature of what is now called Christian ethics. This is not a purely philosophical position but it is the school of moral thinking to which many Protestant scholars belong. While left-wing Christian ethicists adopt a situationist stance and find nothing wrong with divorce, or even adultery that is well motivated,[31] there are opposing voices defending the permanency of marriage. Thus Herbert Waddams thinks that the New Testament teaches that "divorce is a failure of the marriage relationship and therefore to be shunned." [32] He admits that today "the question of the indissolubility of Christian marriage is a disputed point, but it seems to be clearly the teaching of the Anglican and the Roman Catholic Churches." [33] It is not quite right to say, then, that the indissolubility of marriage is "for all practical purposes a conception that is peculiar to the Catholic Church." [34] Millions of people who are not Roman Catholics disapprove of perfect divorce. This is not a philosophical conclusion but a matter of awareness of world opinion, and nothing more need be said about it here. My point is that, if we think of Christian ethics (which really is Protestant moral theology) as something like philosophy, then we must say that this group of thinkers varies from almost complete permissiveness toward divorce to a strong defense of the marital bond.

Of course there are Catholic thinkers who may be regarded as Christian ethicists in the broad sense. Some share the views of left-wing situationists. I really do not know whether Rosemary Ruether thinks of herself as a philosopher. She has argued forcefully that the nature of marriage has changed in recent centuries. Marriage today, she suggests, has lost almost all the productive functions that once centered in the home; it has turned to the cult of children and an intensified love-relation between spouses. With such social changes, she argues, modern marriage has taken on a new meaning—and so has modern divorce. So, she regards divorce as an "escape hatch" which may help to preserve the character of interpersonal fulfillment that she sees as central to modern marriage.[35]

Possibly a more judicious discussion of this matter by a professor of jurisprudence with a strong background in moral philosophy is found in the work of Thomas E. Davitt.[36] He admits the possibility that a well-informed man may not be able to find conclusive evidence in his natural experience and reasoning to support the indissolubility of marriage. In other words, moral philosophy may not be able to solve this problem, but a person who accepts biblical revelation can use that as "higher guidance" in reaching a decision on the permanence of marriage.

In summation of this survey of contemporary philosophical views on marriage, two points should be stressed. First, practically all recent philosophers who discuss marital fidelity dwell upon the importance of interpersonal commitment between spouses. Language may vary from talk about agapistic love to a weak form of mutual appreciation, but there is an almost universal consensus, as I see it, on the central importance of reciprocal trust between married persons. In the second place, most moral philosophers now look upon divorce *a vinculo* as an unfortunate but sometimes necessary termination to a "broken" marriage. There are those who, from motives of religious belief, refuse to approve of perfect divorce. But there are not many prominent contemporary philosophers who support the absolute indissolubility of the marital bond, on the basis of philosophical thinking.

New Features on the Domestic Scene

That there have been changes in the character of marriage in modern times can hardly be doubted, Such developments are primarily the concern of the historian and the social scientist, but the philosopher cannot ignore them and their causes if he is to keep in touch with realities.

First of all, and in spite of what some women's liberationists may say, there has been a decided move toward sexual equality in our day. This is true, I think, not only in theory but in practice. If one looks back to the writings of Aristotle, for instance, one will find an apparently reasonable family man who thinks that his wife and children are his inferiors! In *Politics* we read that "the male is by nature fitter for command than the female" in the human family. A little later Aristotle asks whether slaves can possess moral virtue and he answers that they cannot, for they have no deliberative faculty. Then he adds that women do have deliberative power but "it is without authority." [37] The role of a husband is to command; that of the wife is to obey. In the long history of the subject, only a few philosophers have ventured to challenge this assertion of inequality between the sexes— and these were, oddly, bachelors like Plato and Descartes.

In Thomas Aquinas' only mature treatment of matrimony,[38] there is some effort to see the basic equality of man and woman (as in the argument of *Summa contra Gentiles,* III, 123, that it is unfair to put away an elderly wife), but on the whole St. Thomas does not see woman as man's equal, either in intelligence or in moral capacity. Much the same anti-feminism runs through most philosophy written before the twentieth century. It is prominent in both Kant and Hegel.

Without venturing to document it, let me state my conviction that contemporary philosophy has broken with that notion of inequality. There are hundreds of competent women philosophers now who could not agree with Aristotle, and who disprove by their own achievements the assumption of inequality. In practice, women are not yet given completely equal opportunities in career activities but there is a progressive thrust toward equality in work and in socio-legal standing. The "little-woman" syndrome will soon be a thing of the past.

Second, there has been a tremendous change in the attitudes of people in the Western world toward sex. The sexual revolt has influenced both Catholics and others. Just how extensive and intensive this evolution in mores is remains a matter of dispute.[39] Many well-informed observers think that it is no longer even possible to gain acceptance for rigorous standards of sexual behavior in the present day.[40]

Permissiveness in regard to pre- and extra-marital sexual activities must influence attitudes toward marriage. Not to put too fine a point on it, there is not really much difference between the married state and the non-married state for couples who cohabit and take good care not to produce children. Indeed, under some circumstances the very modern couple may think that it is advantageous not to enter into marriage.

Contraception, as an effective preventive of child-bearing, is recent and socially influential. Very largely it is what has made the sexual revolt possible. But it is also, I think, modifying the character of marriage. My own view is that not only is artificial contraception immoral but also the indiscriminate use of the rhythm method is immoral. This is not a matter of faith, in my case, but of philosophical reasoning.[41] It will be evident, from what was said earlier on the purpose of conjugal society, that I cannot regard a domestic association which deliberately avoids children throughout its duration as a marriage in any real sense. I am quite aware that people may marry who cannot have children, but I do not think that people may marry who can but never will have children.

Concern about population limits is, of course, a very moral feeling. The Malthusian claim, however, is an exaggeration of this concern. World population is not near to saturation. Nevertheless, this phenomenon of getting excited about too many people on earth is a present event; similarly, in the year A.D. 418, thousands got excited about the imminent end of the world. Whether well founded or not, the talk about a population explosion has occasioned some revision of traditional views on marriage. Much the same reaction took place at the end of the eighteenth century, in response to the dire predictions of Thomas Malthus.

Still another feature of recent domestic life that has resulted in changed attitudes toward marriage is the practice of spouses (sometimes one, sometimes both) working at careers outside the home. Many family houses are now vacant throughout the day: neither father, nor mother, nor children remain at home. Even recreation and religious activities take the family from the domestic scene. Many houses are little more than places to sleep. With this development one wonders what sort of family life and conjugal association can grow in the empty home. Even where the mother stays at home, she is alone a good part of her time. Surely there must be more to married life than sharing a common dormitory.

Finally, there is the social phenomenon of over-valuation of financial status. Class distinctions in a Western democracy now depend on the relative income of the family. A wealthy family is upper class! This ridiculous value system is responsible for many negative factors in family life. To increase the domestic wealth the mother tries to earn a separate salary. (It might, indeed, be better to try the Scandinavian experiment of having husband and wife spend alternate periods working at the same job.) On the other hand, the father worries about, and is accused of, failing to provide well for the family. Frequently the children are sent to schools, camps and clubs that are beyond the family means, with a view to building the family image of wealth. Or worse, this is done with the calculated expectation that children will meet better people.

Doubtless there are many other modifiers of the institution of matrimony. Most of those reviewed above have come into play in recent times. They make it difficult to think of marriage in the twentieth century in terms of what it was in the thirteenth century, when canonical regulations were first formulated.

Importance of the Personal Equality of Spouses

It will have become evident from the foregoing that I think modern marriage requires us to agree that a woman is just as important a human being as a man. In fact, I'm ashamed to have to mention this point. It should be obvious that morally speaking there is no reason why man should dominate woman.

Gender differences do exist. It is not the same thing to be a man as to be a woman. Apart from evident physical diversity, there are no doubt basic and ineradicable distinctions in the psychic order. The feminine role in human life cannot be identical with the masculine. However, a woman is a human person, in complete charge of herself morally, equal on the level of ethical personality with the male of her species. This is something that is agreed to, I think, in all forms of contemporary philosophy.

This requires some revision of attitudes on the part of both state and ecclesiastical courts. What is needed is not so much a change of laws as a radical modification of the procedures with which they are applied. As a non-lawyer, I see it as not only reasonable but a matter of strict justice that more women experts be involved in both the preliminary investigation and the adjudication of marital disputes. In both areas women can be quite competent; it is not necessary that they be clerics. Until such a revision of due process in canonical cases is adopted, one-half of the Catholic population is not adequately represented at court. Failure to recognize this is an unfortunate heritage from past prejudices. Let no one misunderstand me: I am saying that natural justice requires that approximately one-half of the experts concerned with matrimonial cases should be women.

Interpersonal Commitment

On the positive side of the picture: What makes a successful marriage? Mutual love is one of the most frequent answers to this question. But love can mean anything from the attraction of iron filings for a magnet to God's own charity. The first is too little to cement a marriage; the second is too much to expect. Romantic love (in the sense of emotional attachment) has indeed been over-emphasized in modern times. Sexual attraction is a part of the normal tie between spouses, but it is neither the whole bond, nor is it always a necessary element. A more high-minded love (in the precise language of Thomism, a habit of will rather than a function of sensory appetite) is more obviously central in most good marriages. But I am not certain that agapistic love (except in the broad sense of good will for all human creatures of God) is really required for success in the matrimonial union. What is really needed, I think, is a sense of intimate interpersonal commitment between spouses. They must agree on what they will to achieve together. In some cases, husband and wife may live well together—even if one or both be chiefly motivated by an awareness of duty. This is a minimum bond but it is frequently enough. If spouses are also animated by what Aristotle called the love of friendship, this is much better. Each should be willing the good of the other and the common good that is appropriate to family life in the fullest sense. It is easier to do one's duty when one likes doing it. Again, as Marcel said, if spouses can be united by some form of spiritual fidelity, rooted in the supernatural order, that is an optimum ideal. Clearly this is beyond the reach of philosophy not illuminated by faith.

What this means practically has been indicated by many writers. People need better training to live together in marriage. It is not a question of more sex education but of greater information on the meaning, the obligations, the privileges and the difficulties of domestic life. Such education cannot be given in a few easy instructions by a person who has spent no part of his adult life in a family. Much preparation for marriage was in former times gained from experience in growing up in one's home with parents. Nowadays we may have to think of more formal studies. The ordinary marriage course in college is better than nothing but it is not as effective as it could be and it does not reach the non-college people who need it. Perhaps we should be giving more thought to adequate preparation for marriage and less to what may be done for unsuccessful marriages.

Inter-personal Conflict in Marriage

Disagreements, arguments, husband-and-wife fights are part of the marriage picture. Anyone who does not know this should avoid this subject. In one sense these disputes can be destructive: they may break down the mutual trust that is essential to a viable conjugal union. The negative effects of marital conflicts may be uppermost in the minds of many marriage counselors and divorce lawyers.

Yet there can be a positive value, a good for the marriage, that may arise out of such quarreling. Much depends on the education, the degree of sophistication, and the prior preparation for life of each married partner. One of the things that critics of liberal education forget, when they say that it does not prepare one to earn a living, is that there is more to life than working. There is the knowledge of how to live well, particularly when one is free from work.

Contemporary phenomenology really has something useful to say about personal conflicts. This is found in the teaching on the positive value of the "obstacle." A thorough explanation is given in the work of René Le Senne, a Catholic philosopher who is not well known to English readers.[42] He sees a block, an opposition, as an event which makes possible an ascent to a higher good. Without some struggle human life would be drab and meaningless. Developing this same theme, Marcel says that it is not necessarily a bad thing for two young people in love to be separated from each other for a time.

Time and separation are not merely obstacles, resistant to their purposes, here; rather what resists them is used, and a functional value is conferred on it; such value consists in making possible what we may call an inner confrontation.[43]

I think Marcel means that a young couple hardly know each other (are "present" to each other) until they have had their first quarrels.

Jean-Paul Sartre discusses the example of a person who looks ahead to a mountain crag. He may see it as an obstacle, as something which can, or cannot, be overcome. He may regard the peak as something that takes effort to climb but which will enable him to see farther when it has been conquered.[44] Adversity need not be viewed as evil.

Many difficulties that lead to divorce proceedings are minor in the mind of an impartial observer. Much depends on the frame of mind with which difficulties are faced. It is infinitely better to provide means whereby spouses can turn their disputes into peaks to be conquered, rather than to concentrate on how to end their marriage because of misunderstanding and conflict.

Legal Justice, Equity, and "Juris-Prudence"

Sometimes it is healthy to see ourselves through the eyes of an able critic. Nikolai Berdyaev admits that "marriage as a sacrament, mystical marriage, is by its very meaning eternal and indissoluble." But he also thinks that many marriages have no mystical meaning and do not reach the spiritual level. Hence, he concludes that the prohibition of divorce "is based upon a legalistic interpretation of Christianity." Then Berdyaev says:

To prohibit divorce, as the Roman Catholic Church in particular insists on doing, is one of the most cruel things that can be done to human beings, forcing them to live in an atmosphere of falsity, hypocrisy and tyranny and to profane their most intimate feelings.[45]

These strong words may be taken with a grain of salt but they should make us take thought about this so-called "legalism" of the Latin Church. Are we really following what is best in our tradition?

It has been shown by an expert in Canon Law that Roman Catholic canonists gradually changed the meaning of justice from the thirteenth century onward, so that eventually justice in the highest sense, which is equity, came to be confused with mercy.[46] As a result of this extraordinary development, an excessive devotion to legal justice did come about. This evolution has not been good for the Church and it has certainly not helped married people.

It was a commonplace in thirteenth-century *Summa*'s for the treatise on laws to distinguish several kinds of justice: these were the subjective parts of this virtue. I shall refer briefly to Thomas Aquinas on this matter, but much the same teaching will be found in the Franciscan thinkers of this time. Aquinas insisted that all human justice is imperfect in comparison with divine justice.[47] Divine justice here means what God knows to be right—not what any human court, civil or ecclesiastical, judges.

In the second place, Aquinas thought that there are two kinds of justice in general: these are equity (*epieikeia*) and legal justice.[48] Of these two, equity is justice in the highest and most perfect sense, while legal justice is a derivative from equity and it is expressed in ordinances that cover ordinary matters. Unusual cases, exceptions under legal justice, are to be judged in terms of justice-as-equity. Since there is no way of codifying equity judgments (each is a unique statement of what is right in this one case), it is clear that laws (universal regulations) are but expressions of legal justice. In simple words, it is not always the just thing to follow the letter of the law.

Matrimonial cases, for instance, that can be adjudicated under codified law are the easy ones. Other marriage disputes may involve unusual circumstances (I suspect that many do), and the point is that justice may not be served in such cases by adhering to the provisions of legal justice. This is not legal relativism; this is the common teaching of the great Catholic theologians of the thirteenth century. Equity is the nearest approach to the justice of God. Now it is not easy to be a judge in equity; one must think harder and risk more than the judge who sticks to legal justice.

An equity judge needs a very special skill to see what is an exceptional case (this is the habit known to the medieval theologians as *gnome*). He must acquire an intellectual quality that gives him an ability to decide what is right (the *justum*) —even in a case that is not covered by ordinance. What this second skill amounts to is "juris-prudence." It is not the theory of law (which has by some error come to be called "jurisprudence"), but it is a special skill in judging concrete problems of justice in accord, not with law (*lex*) but with the essence of rightness (*jus*).

If this part of our wise legal heritage could be recovered,

the adjudication of canonical cases might be more flexible and more just. There is something wrong when a judge knows and feels that in following the rules he is reaching an unfair judgment. Perhaps a better understanding of equity would help us to avoid criticism as legalists and rigorists.

NOTES

1. If one separates "theology" from a special set of *credibilia*, then it becomes but another name for philosophy.
2. Helmut Thielicke, *The Ethics of Sex*, trans. J. W. Doberstein (New York: Harper & Row, 1964), pp. 130ff., clearly explains the Lutheran position: the New Testament does not say that matrimony is a sacrament, since "marriage existed before Christ and also among the heathen." Martin Luther made a point of being married in his own home to indicate that he did not consider it an ecclesiastical event. On the age and universality of monogamous marriage, see Crane Brinton, *A History of Western Morals* (New York: Harcourt, Brace, 1959), pp. 34-36.
3. The notion that mutual love is essential to marriage is comparatively recent. Paul Weiss argues that a genuine family life requires appreciation, something "a little less vivid than affection," but not love in the romantic sense: *Our Public Life* (Bloomington: Indiana University Press, 1959), pp. 231-235.
4. Apart from any religious consideration, Herbert Doms was philosophically in error, I think, in saying. "The first and most immediate object of marriage is, then, the fulfillment of two human beings": *The Meaning of Marriage*, trans. George Sayer (New York: Sheed & Ward, 1939), p. 38.
5. Kenneth Keniston, "Youth and Violence: The Contexts of Moral Crisis," in *Moral Education*, edited by Nancy F. and Theodore R. Sizer (Cambridge, Mass.: Harvard University Press, 1970), p. 118. Keniston is a professor of psychiatric pychology and the author of *Young Radicals* (New York: Harcourt, Brace, 1968).
6. *Marriage and Society* (New York: John de Graff, 1955), p. 161.
7. *Psychology and Morals, An Analysis of Character* (London: Methuen, 1949); cited in John Wilson, *Logic and Sexual Morality* (Harmondsworth: Penguin, 1965), p. 271. Wilson (pp. 271-272), cites several other psychologists of sex who share this view.
8. "At no time is consciousness capable of growth in being without being initially beholden to its dialogue with another consciousness": J. Nabert, *Elements for an Ethic*, trans. W. J. Petrek (Evanston: Northwestern University Press, 1969), p. 139; see the whole of Chapter 9: "Experience of the One in the Interchange of Minds."
9. A very well informed Swiss Protestant writer, Roger Mehl, suggests

that Marcel's thought should be more exploited by Catholic moralists because it offers what Mehl considers a remedy for excessive dualism (of soul and body) in the Catholic tradition. See *Catholic Ethics and Protestant Ethics,* trans. J. H. Farley (Philadelphia: Westminster Press, 1970), pp. 86-87.

10. *Creative Fidelity,* trans. Robert Rostal (New York: Farrar, Strauss & Co., 1964), p. 158.

11. On this concept of "presence," cf. *ibid.,* p. 153.

12. *Ibid.,* p. 158.

13. *Ibid.,* pp. 18-21.

14. *Ibid.,* p. 101.

15. For a quick survey of analytic ethics, see my *History of Ethics* (New York: Doubleday, 1968), Chapter XVII.

16. J. F. Dedek (not an analyst but well aware of contemporary thinking on such problems), writes in *Contemporary Sexual Morality* (New York: Sheed & Ward, 1971), p. 82: "Only an absolute being can effect something that is absolute. A vow is a promise about the future, but many of the contingencies of the future remain hidden from us. The Church or any human authority cannot make a law which binds absolutely in all possible situations, precisely because a human authority cannot forsee all possible situations. Neither can an individual legislate for himself, as it were, in any absolute way." Father Dedek is thinking primarily of ordination promises.

17. See John R. Searle, "How to Derive 'Ought' from 'Is'," in *Philosophical Review,* 73 (1964), pp. 43-58, and the critical response in R. M. Hare, "The Promising Game," in *Revue Internationale de Philosophie,* 70 (1964), pp. 398-412; both are reprinted in *Theories of Ethics,* edited by Philippa Foot (London: Oxford University Press, 1967), pp. 101-127.

18. See his *Logic and Sexual Morality, op. cit.,* pp. 268-272.

19. The quotation is from Oswald Schwarz, *The Psychology of Sex* (Harmondsworth: Penguin, 1956), pp. 218-219.

20. Patrick Devlin, *The Enforcement of Morals* (London: Oxford University Press, 1965), p. 62, in the Earl Grey Memorial Lecture (1963), entitled: "Morals and the Law of Marriage." For H. L. A. Hart's stronger position, see his *Punishment and Responsibility* (London: Oxford University Press, 1968).

21. Cf. Roger Hazelton, "Humanism and Humanitarianism," in *Dictionary of Christian Ethics,* edited by John Macquarrie (Philadelphia: Westminster Press, 1967), pp. 157-159.

22. On this point the position of B. F. Skinner (who is a humanist), in his *Beyond Freedom and Dignity* (New York: Knopf, 1971), is a-typical. Skinner has room for no kind of human liberty.

23. Blackham, "Moral Theory and Moral Education," in *Moral Problems in Contemporary Society. Essays in Humanistic Ethics,* edited by Paul Kurtz (Englewood Cliffs: Prentice-Hall, 1969), p. 248. See also the article, "Humanist Ethics and the Meaning of Human Dignity," by Abraham Edel (*ibid.,* pp. 227-240), who is one of the ablest advocates of humanism.

24. For a study of the world-wide influence of atheistic humanism,

see Henri de Lubac, *Le Drame de l'Humanisme athée* (1959); trans. as *The Drama of Atheist Humanism*, by Edith M. Riley (London-New York: Sheed & Ward, 1950).

25. Most representative is *The Human Venture in Sex, Love, and Marriage* (New York: Association Press, 1949), reprinted in 1959; see Chapter 4: "Roots of Creative Marriage," pp. 116-143.

26. Cf. Eugene Kamenka, *Marxism and Ethics* (London: Macmillan, 1969), and Richard T. De George, *Soviet Ethics and Morality* (Ann Arbor: University of Michigan Press), 1969. Luther J. Binkley, *Conflict of Ideals. Changing Values in Western Society* (New York: Van Nostrand-Reinhold), 1969, pp. 44-81, provides a short survey.

27. See my article, "Recent Trends in Ethics," in *The New Scholasticism*, 44 (1970), pp. 405-410, for more details.

28. Wolfgang G. Friedmann, *Law in a Changing Society* (Berkeley: University of California Press), 1959, p. 212. The point is discussed in Devlin, *Enforcement of Morals, op. cit.*, p. 79.

29. For the whole Code, see De George, *op. cit.*, p. 83.

30. *Ibid.*, pp. 96-97: "The Soviet emphasis on family stability seems based primarily on concern for the children."

31. Joseph Fletcher's views are too well known to require exposition here. For recent dialogue, see *The Situation Ethics Debate*, edited by Harvey Cox (Philadelphia: Westminster Press, 1968).

32. "Marriage," in *Dictionary of Christian Ethics* (1967), p. 206.

33. *Ibid.*, p. 207; in his article, "Divorce," *idem*, p. 91, Canon Waddams plainly states that divorce *a vinculo* is "incompatible with the indissolubility of marriage as it has been traditionally held' in Western Christendom." He notes the more permissive practice of the Eastern Orthodox Church.

34. See J. F. Dedek, *op. cit.*, p. 139.

35. Rosemary Ruether, "Divorce: No Longer Unthinkable," in *Commonweal* 84 (April 14, 1967), pp. 117-118. The passage is discussed in R. L. Cunningham, *Situationism and the New Morality* (New York: Appleton-Century-Crofts, 1970), p. 19.

36. *Ethics in the Situation* (New York: Appleton-Century-Crofts, 1970), pp. 160-164.

37. Aristotle, *Politica*, I, cc. 12-13, 1259a39–1260a12.

38. *Summa contra Gentiles*, III, cc. 122-126; see my translation in *On the Truth of the Catholic Faith* (New York: Doubleday, 1956), Part II, pp. 142-156.

39. I am inclined to think that P. A. Sorokin in *The American Sex Revolution* (Boston: Porter Sargent, 1956) exaggerates the extent of the revolt. But my own forty-year experience with college classes in ethics suggests that the sex attitudes of even fifteen years ago are no longer in vogue today. Now few things are taboo.

40. See the rather moderate book by J. G. Milhaven, *Toward a New Catholic Morality* (New York: Doubleday, 1970), and the previously cited work by Dedek. In the symposium, *Sexual Ethics and Christian Responsibility*, edited by John C. Wynn (New York: Association Press, 1970), both Catholic contributors are critical of traditional Catholic views on sex.

41. See my chapter, "An Ethical Consideration of Artificial Contraception," in *What Modern Catholics Think About Birth Control,* edited by Wm. Birmingham (New York: Signet, 1964), pp. 15-28.

42. See Le Senne, *Obstacle et Valeur* (Paris: Aubier, 1934).

43. G. Marcel, *Creative Fidelity, op. cit.,* p. 73.

44. J.-P. Sartre, *Being and Nothingness,* trans. Hazel E. Barnes (New York: Philosophical Library, 1956), p. 482.

45. N. Berdyaev, *The Destiny of Man,* trans. Natalie Duddington (New York: Harper & Row, 1960), p. 234.

46. See Charles Lefebvre, "Natural and Canonical Equity," in *Natural Law Forum,* VIII (1963), pp. 122-136. (At the time this was written, Msgr. Lefebvre was an auditor of the Roman Rota.)

47. S. Thomae Aquinatis, *Expositio in Job,* cap. 23, lectio 1; see my *Ethics in Crisis* (New York: Bruce-Macmillan, 1966), p. 126, for the full text in English. Cf. S. Thomae Aquinatis, *In Psalmos Davidis Expositio,* 25, 1.

48. *Summa Theologiae,* II-II, q. 120, art. 2, c.

John Charles Wynn

Prevailing and Countervailing Trends in the Non-Catholic Churches

W inds of change never blow in one consistent direction only. In the ecclesiastical storms of our day, as surely as in the weather reports, there are prevailing winds and countervailing winds. Nor does any church today escape the *Sturm und Drang* of the disturbance. This essay will isolate samplings of Protestant and Orthodox denominations and present data concerning their struggle with the challenge to the ideal of indissoluble marriage in contemporary American life.

No church denies that the Christian faith establishes a standard of indissolubility for marriage. Yet no church fails to allow for arrangements whereby a marriage can be dissolved. The concept of indissolubility has, now for a generation, been interpreted with widening latitude. The moral rights identified in exceptional cases, and duly considered among all the church bodies in this nation, have opened a debate that produces strenuous arguments for some amelioration in church law. In a day when Tillichian theology has reinforced concern for the person as well as respect for the principle in Christian ethics, the various denominations have all found it essential to balance their statutes with consideration of inter-personal relationships as well.

Indissolubility is of the essence of marriage, an element inherent in God's intention for mankind. And the vow of fidelity and perseverence in the covenant of marriage is central to the union. Constancy to that pledge, despite the challenges and difficulties of family life, is the logical expectation of a Christian marriage. As Emil Brunner puts it:

Neither adultery in the crude meaning of the word, nor impotence nor sterility, nor a serious defect or crime, constitutes in itself an ethical "reason for divorce." A human being of strong faith can, under some circumstances, inwardly rise above all this, and can maintain the marriage in spite of all these extraordinary burdens. . . . The moral presuppositions of divorce in contradistinction to the legal presuppositions can be codified into no law.[1]

For the most profound conviction about indissolubility we look to the Mormons; members of The Church of Jesus Christ Latter Day Saints believe in marriage for eternity, not just until death parts them in this world. Other religious groups, however, usually affirm that death releases the surviving partner from marital vows. No longer is digamy (remarriage following the spouse's death) judged illicit. And in one way or another church courts allow that numerous other circumstances sever the relationship.

All churches disapprove of divorce, but they vary to the degree that they condemn it. William J. Goode, author of several sociological studies of divorce, deplores the lack of exact data regarding religious correlations with divorce (the U.S. census survey, for example, asks no questions about religion which could be cross-tabulated with data on marriage).[2] However, he has gleaned from statistical samplings elsewhere a scale of general findings about the divorce experience of persons from different religious bodies. Jews who marry Jews and Catholics who marry Catholics have the lowest divorce rates, he concludes. Protestants wed to Protestants come next. But whenever both husband and wife are in the same church, the rates of Catholics, Protestants and Jews tend to cluster closely on the graph. Those couples with no religious affiliation, on the other hand, have the highest divorce rate. Next highest are those in mixed marriages from two variant faith traditions.

Even so, much depends on the individual relationship of a given husband and wife; obviously their personal situation can alter these generalizations. Church membership alone does not determine whether a person will divorce. (The devoutness of an adherent is a more influential factor than mere membership.) Religion is but one of the numerous sociological factors that bear on the matter. Divorce, regardless of whether we like it or not, is built into the social structure. Its causes are numerous and complex. They stem from the availability of ready divorce, from economic reversals, even from family tradition where broken marriage is common; but these are only a few of the associated circumstances. Perhaps the hardest for Christians to face is that many couples divorce simply because they no longer wish to live with one another.[3]

Divorce, despite its obstacles and expense, has increased in recent years. For some persons it has become a more realistic relief for marital tensions than any alternative they can see. The rise in the divorce rate has been significantly correlated with the lessened disapproval toward divorce in society. The increasing ability of the woman to support herself, the near certainty that a new mate can be found, the support of one's friends through a divorce: these have exacerbated a rising divorce rate. Indeed the impulse to break out from an ill-fitting union rather than work it through has become so prevalent that without some societal sanctions the divorce statistic would be even worse. But we have contrived a number of social safeguards for persons to marry homogamously those mates similar to themselves and from congenial backgrounds, for couples to lower their expectations of romance and satisfaction after some years of marriage, and for some disagreements to be accepted as unimportant and tolerable. In the conditioning of these sanctions the churches have played no small role. The clergy have attempted to infuse not only theological principles but also social realism into marital expectations through premarital education and counseling.

That the churches have enjoyed limited success in their efforts at stabilizing marriages can be seen in current history. Alfred E. Kinsey may have been correct in his assertion that "there is nothing more important in a marriage than a determination that it shall persist" after his study of nearly 9,000 marital histories.[4] But John A. Siramaki criticizes the churches themselves for weakening this determination. Churchly tolerance for divorce, he avers, has abetted the increase in divorce rates.[5] Wayne E. Oates notes that although 90% of all weddings are performed in churches, the great majority (71%) have received no pre-marital guidance from the churches.[6] Rosemary Ruether must be correct in her contention that "the church and its ministry must share in the guilt and hardness of heart associated with divorce." [7]

Nearly all church bodies exhibit a pronounced move away from legalism in their divorce pronouncements today. Biblical scholarship has underscored the widely held opinion that when Jesus spoke about marriage, divorce and remarriage in the Synoptic Gospels he was issuing a call to repentance rather than setting up a new law code or replacing old statutes with new.[8]

Major Protestant denominations, e.g., Presbyterians, Lutherans, Methodists, and Episcopalians, show clear signs of decreasing the type of adversary litigation their church standards had once used when they sought to identify one spouse as guilty, the other as innocent. No longer do they so strictly confine their consideration of divorce to cases of adultery and desertion. Rather they note other evidence of marital breakdown in which the husband and wife are both culpable.

Two such different observers as Rosemary Ruether and Emil

Brunner have commented trenchantly on this trend. In her survey of the Catholic tradition, she contends that while marriage in the modern age has moved from a legalistic relationship to an inter-personal relationship, the church is not geared to this change:

The traditional ecclesiastical discipline on marriage has become untenable because it no longer has anything to do with the present social reality of marriage. Stemming from a period when marriage was really a public institution, it views the marital bond in legal terms and not in interpersonal terms. . . . Only when it is clear that this law understands marriage as a legal contract and not as a personal community is it possible to understand why it considers the bond to remain in force long after the relationship has terminated.[9]

Brunner sums up a section on divorce in his work on dogmatics with this sharp word:

Even in matters of marriage God is more merciful than the usual theological ethic, and to learn to know this mercy of God aright would be a surer means of defense against libertinism than the legalism which so proudly plumes itself upon its "seriousness" and its "freedom from compromise." Were it not for the fact that pastoral practice has at times acted with far more insight than the official doctrine would have permitted, the diaster would have attained greater proportions, and the crisis would have supervened much earlier. It is the curse of "Christian morality" that it always regards the most legalistic view as the "most serious."[10]

This movement away from legalistic interpretation, indeed, characterizes most of the main-line Protestant denominations today. Challenged both by a theological conviction that indissolubility in marriage is the will of God, and that contemporary couples suffer anew from hardness of heart as well as social conditions that biblical man never knew, the churches are coming to terms with a new ethic that, at this writing, is obviously still in transition to something that hopefully will be better.

Presbyterian and Reformed Churches

Just 100 years after the Council of Trent, the Westminster Divines formulated their *Confession of Faith,* an extensive credal statement that has served the Presbyterian and Reformed system (including the related Congregational churches and The United Church of Christ) throughout their history. Like Tridentine statements, those of the Westminster Confession have also been updated in recent years. The sole reasons for which divorce was originally allowed were adultery and desertion "as if the offending party were dead." [11]

It is lawful for the innocent party to sue for a divorce, and, after the divorce, to marry another . . . yet nothing but adultery or such willful desertion as can no way be remedied by the Church or civil magistrate, is cause sufficient of dissolving the bond of marriage: wherein a public and orderly course of proceeding is to be observed. [12]

Behind the theological reasoning of much Presbyterian-type government is the fine French hand of that ecclesiastical lawyer, John Calvin. He hated divorce; he was convinced that God had established marriage to be monogamous and indissoluble. Convinced also that the fall of mankind corrupted the marital state as well as every other segment of living, he reluctantly came to regard divorce as the severance of a hopelessly broken and hostile marriage. This same candid understanding of indissolubility as the will of God—and divorce as the consequence of man's creatureliness shows up in two sections of the United Presbyterian Church's *Constitution:*

God has ordained that a man and woman may enter together into the estate of marriage, pledging their love and promising fidelity each to the other, as long as they both shall live. [13]

Recognizing the action of the state [to grant divorce] as an accomplished fact, the church's responsibility for education and counsel before marriage also extends to any special problems after divorce.[14]

In a similar vein The Presbyterian Church of Canada has noted that "the essential nature of marriage is that it is an indissoluble union of two people, joined together in a one-flesh relationship. . . . The fact of marriage then does not include divorce. If there is the possibility of receiving a 'Certificate of Divorce' this is not the original and perfect will of God." [15]

The modern theologian with the greatest influence on all Reformed churches is, of course, Karl Barth. His theological ethics expounds this same indissolubility-but-broken-marriage paradox: "The saying of Jesus cannot be reversed: 'What God hath not joined together, let man put asunder'. . . . Man can and perhaps in certain situations must dissolve it, because without the divine foundation which alone could make it indissoluble, it lacks genuine and essential permanence because it is not in the judgment of God a tenable marriage." [16]

All of the churches of the Presbyterian and Reformed family stress the requirement of penitence and forgiveness after a marriage has been broken, however, before any pastor could give consideration to officiating at the nuptial ceremony for remarriage. Thus, for example, the Presbyterian Church of the United States: "The remarriage of divorced persons may be sanctioned by the Church in keeping with the redemptive Gospel of Christ, when sufficient penitence for sin and failure is evident, and a firm purpose of and endeavor after Christian marriage is manifested." [17]

This repeated concern that the Gospel take precedence over the law in New Testament theology, here implied, is a modern emphasis. Most Protestant churches concur in their recent statements concerning the place of the law in marriage and divorce. And certainly the roots for such an interpretation reach back to Martin Luther. Yet a legalistic, even a vindictive spirit had characterized earlier years of church discipline among these very denominations.

And that same understanding of the Gospel's precedence

over the law is evident in the numerous church statements, among them that Jesus was enunciating a principle rather than a law in his teachings on this subject. This repugnance toward making church courts into trial courts of marital grief is obvious in a spate of resolutions. With a clearer understanding of pastoral theology, today's clergy are reluctant simply to label one party guilty and the other innocent in a marriage broken on scriptural grounds. They are aware that an act of infidelity is a marital offense; they are likewise aware that there are many subtler but also deadly offenses in marital relationships. Together with numerous theologians through the centuries, they recognize that neither adultery nor willful desertion automatically brings about the dissolution of a marriage. In the complete reappraisal of their denominational standards on this topic in the recent past, Presbyterian and Reformed groups have, as one of their publications phrased it, affirmed that it is the "duty of the church to minister the Gospel to those involved in broken marriages, proclaiming judgment and the salvation of Christ and providing for them a reconciling fellowship." [18]

The Methodist Position

In common with other Protestant denominations The United Methodist Church (recently merged with The Evangelical United Brethren) understands marriage to be a sacred covenant relationship under God. In a definitive statement, "The Church and The Family," passed as a general resolution at The General Conference of 1968, the Methodists approached the problem of broken marriage and the possibility of remarriage pastorally:

Divorce should never be taken lightly; it is such a serious matter that it should be considered only after every possible resolution has been explored. We recognize that divorce is not the answer to problems that cause it, but is symptomatic of deeper difficulties.

The church stands ready to help persons considering divorce to face the difficulties involved, and, if possible, to overcome them. The church will surround with love and fellowship those persons experiencing broken marriage, and, through pastoral care and counseling, help them utilize the resources of the Christian faith to make satisfactory adjustments to a new life.

Remarriage after divorce should be considered only after sufficient time has passed for a person to overcome the hurt, resolve the difficulties of the past, and become prepared to enter a new marriage as a covenant relationship.[19]

This resolution, coming out of one of the largest Protestant bodies, represents something of the mainstream of thinking in non-Roman churches during recent years. Such thinking tends now to be less doctrinal, more pastoral. And this resolution appears to have met head-on one difficult problem; it avoids an arbitrary time definition for persons awaiting remarriage following divorce. Instead of prescribing a minimal one-year waiting period for a couple following a divorce decree, the Methodists in convention spoke of "sufficient time" to prepare for a new marriage and to establish a firm Christian home.

In Methodist tradition, marriage is viewed as ordained by God from the orders of creation, a covenant relation for life. This expectation of permanence is realistically assessed in denominational pronouncements as more possible for some couples to achieve than others. They are convinced that marital failure is a reality that must be faced with understanding and love. Husbands and wives in conflict are expected to seek competent help from qualified sources. And while in such counseling they are to continue in marriage, not primarily because of the pressures of society or of personal satisfactions, but because each accepts marriage as a sacred covenant relationship under God. This denomination may have gone farther than others in implying permission for divorce when in their 1972 General Convention they added this note: "In marriages where the partners are, even after thoughtful consideration and counsel, estranged beyond reconciliation, we recognize divorce and the right of divorced persons to remarry." [20]

The Lutheran Churches

Martin Luther, ever outspoken and earthy, had begun his religious life believing in the Catholic position on marriage as a sacrament, but came to reject this on biblical grounds and later denied that the Church should hold jurisdiction over marriages. Marriage, he taught, is an outward and secular matter, and subject to the authorities like food and clothing, house and land. The deserted spouse, he believed, can avail himself of the Pauline privilege and can remarry; for the marital bond is broken not only by adultery, but also by desertion and by unbelief.[21]

This same note of candor and realism is reflected in the recent pronouncements of Lutheran bodies in this country. "Divorce is a reality among sinful mankind," the American Lutheran Church declared in 1956; "the legal dissolution of a marriage sometimes is the lesser of evils." Problems are normal to marriage, this church affirmed in its convention of that year. Indeed, "human frailty being so great, not every marriage succeeds. Jesus understood this. He did not condemn or drive away a divorced person." [22] That Lutherans are hardly alone in this reference to compassion is seen in a word of Bernard Häring in a work he had written some four years before his chapter appeared in this volume. The sacrament of peace should not be withheld from those who have failed at marriage, he held in *Shalom: The Sacrament of Reconciliation*. For it is not to be construed "as a reward for complete success, but a remedy to be applied in life's difficulties and struggles. . . . I cannot imagine that Christ would have sent them away without a kind word of peace." [23]

Indeed The Lutheran Church in America, a sister denomination, went so far as to affirm recently that there may be situations in which divorce is a more responsible Christian

action than remaining together in an anguished and under-
mined marital relationship. In fact, given adequate pastoral
guidance, "a clear understanding of the dynamics which led
to the breakdown of the first union helps a person prepare
more adequately for the second." [24]

A similar realistic approach is seen in the concerns of the
more conservative branch, The Lutheran Church, Missouri
Synod. H. G. Coiner writing in *The Concordia Theological
Monthly,* notes that in New Testament theology "there is to be no
divorce among those who are committed to God's will for marriage and *who are able to maintain the marriage.*" [25]

Yet these references cannot be construed to mean that
Lutherans are soft on divorce. Instead they base their words
on theological conviction and the doctrine of reconciliation.
Marriage, for them, has traditionally been rooted in the
orders of creation. "Marriage exists within a world which is
characterized by alienation from God and from fellow man,
and therefore is affected by the sinfulness of man. Nevertheless, being part of God's creating and sustaining order,
marriage as an institution continues to exist under God's goodness
and protection." [26]

By the same token, Christian marriage is not dissoluble.
As Carl F. Reuss phrases it in a statement given informal,
joint approval both by the American Lutherans and The
Missouri Synod, the oneness of husband and wife "marked
by unwavering fidelity of husband and wife" is compared in
Scripture to the oneness of Christ and his Church.[27]

Likewise the L.C.A. officially defines "marriage as a covenant of one man and one woman in a personal and sexual
union . . . mutual commitment to life-long faithfulness." [28]

This emphasis on the indissoluble nature of Christian marriage is blended with a typical Lutheran conviction concerning freedom under the law. Over and again they remind
themselves, as The Missouri Synod statement puts it, that
"we have freedom in Christ (Gal. 5:1), not being bound by
the edicts of men." This point is hardly neglected by any
theologians of the Lutheran tradition, beginning with the

Reformer himself. Helmut Thielicke is persuaded that marriage, being an order of creation, dare not be interpreted legalistically,[29] and Günther Bornkamm avers that the precept of the primitive Church cannot be elevated to the status of a law established once and for all, any more than the primitive Church itself converted the words of Jesus into such a law.[30]

Thus buttressed by theology, Lutherans are able to confirm that Jesus spoke no word by which a man or woman might whitewash his divorce into a righteous act, yet that the Bible nowhere offers either specific permission for the remarriage of divorced persons or anywhere lists divorce as unforgivable.[31]

The Anglicans

The Anglican commonwealth of churches is related family-style through The Lambeth Conference, which exerts a world-wide influence on standards. On this continent we have The Anglican Church of Canada and the Protestant Episcopal Church in the U.S.A. For such national churches *The Book of Common Prayer* is a definitive and cementing force, and The Lambeth Conference remains a reminder of the tradition they share. Although the regional churches may lay down varying applications of how priests are to deal with the canons regarding marriage, they are unlikely to forget Resolution 67:

The Conference affirms as our Lord's principle and standard of marriage a life-long and indissoluble union "for better, for worse" of one man and one woman to the exclusion of all others on either side, and calls on all Christian people to maintain and bear witness to this standard.[32]

These churches, however, have no more escaped the winds of change than the others under study in this book, and their commissions have also been at work on questions of marriage, divorce, and remarriage. The Episcopal Church, for example, has at work a Joint Commission on the Church in Human Affairs which is to report on possible revisions in the marriage canons at The General Convention of 1973. Clergy who have pressed for new pastoral standards have, in particular, drawn attention to three problems with which they currently deal in marital cases. First, there is some ambiguity about who is technically eligible to apply for a judgment of marital status ("the member in good standing"). Second, clarity is needed regarding those applications for judgment of status where no subsequent union is in prospect. Third, the present rigid requirement that clergy may not perform the service of holy matrimony for church members, until one year has elapsed since a previous marriage was dissolved, has worked some hardship in certain instances. The evident direction of changes coming in Episcopal canon law can be measured by the steps already taken in the sister denomination north of the border.

The Anglican Church of Canada since 1967 has provided for an Ecclesiastical Matrimonial Commission in each diocese. Application for permission to remarry in the church is made at the parish level, and then, after investigation, forwarded to this commission. Permission to remarry may (or may not) then be granted when the case is judged against a rigorous set of standards. These include a concern for earnestness shown for reconciliation in the first marriage, the stability of the new marriage, the cause of the former marital breakdown, arrangements for minor children from a previous union, *et al.* A commentary provided with the new canons adds this word: "This represents a major change in our Anglican discipline and thought. . . . The General Synod, by its approval of this change, has brought divorce and the obligation of the church to minister to the divorced right into the main aisle of every parish church." [33]

Derrick Sherwin Bailey, a foremost moral theologian in The Church of England, has commented that many have found his church "somewhat tender" in the matter of prohibition of remarriages.[34] He points out that *The Book of*

Common Prayer does not pronounce marriage as indissoluble, but declares scripturally that whom God has joined together no man may put asunder. His interpretation is that "the vow and covenant" made between a man and a woman binds them, until death, but that this does not of itself bring into existence a relation that is indissoluble. The vow, he writes, has no ontological consequences, but simply expresses a serious and considered intention and embodies the terms on which they propose to contract marriage. He appeals to the teachings of Jesus in Matthew's Gospel:

Although our Lord did not expressly pronounce marriage indissoluble in the impossibilist sense, he may have prohibited remarriage on disciplinary grounds. . . . Jesus' teaching may legitimately be interpreted as laying upon husband and wife a moral obligation to preserve absolute fidelity to one another, while not disallowing divorce and remarriage where special circumstances can be held to justify them. That is to say, he condemns putting away for arbitrary or trivial reasons, especially with a view to a second union, but by implication does not prohibit the husband from seeking or consenting to dissolution of a marriage for any grave cause, such as the law allowed.[35]

It was an English bishop, The Right Reverend John A. T. Robinson, who gave legalistic and absolutistic canons their gruffest shaking in his *Honest To God,* a 1963 publication that drew upon the theological writings of Paul Tillich, Dietrich Bonhoeffer, and Rudolph Bultmann. Challenging the traditional thought that ecclesiastical canons and Christian morals have a supra-naturalistic support, he examines divorce in "the new morality." In the supra-natural position, he concedes, divorce is quite literally, and not merely morally, impossible. Marriage then is not simply indissoluble; it is indelible. However, he doubts that many today believe doctrinally that "marriages are made in heaven." Indissolubility, the bishop argues, can mean that marriages ought not to be dissolved, or that they ought never to be dissolved, or even that they cannot be dissolved. The legalistic position that

God has laid down unchangeable laws which never shall be broken is the stand that bishops are expected to defend, he admits, and it is profoundly shocking for him to appear to contradict. Yet Jesus' teaching on marriage, he notes, is not a new law prescribing that divorce is always and in every case the greater of two evils (whereas Moses said there are some cases in which it was not). It is saying that love, utterly unconditional love, admits of no accommodation.[36]

The final word on indissolubility has not been spoken by the Anglicans. Given their contemporary theological labors on this issue, it is evident that this word is still some distance away.

The Greek Orthodox Churches

The major non-Roman church tradition in which Christian marriage is considered a sacrament is the Orthodox. For the Greek Orthodox churchmen, marriage has a divine foundation and conveys grace through outward signs. This sacrament is considered indissoluble; both Scripture and the tradition of the church support this dogma. Yet they take sharp exception to the Roman Catholic view that marriage is *absolutely* indissoluble.[37]

Divorce is permissible under circumstances for grave causes which make married life impossible. The sole cause for dissolution is fornication. But a plot against one's life by the spouse, procuring or inducing an abortion, sexual impotence, insanity, the monastic state, abandonment, fraudulent or forced marriage: these have been causes for divorce cases granted by the ecclesiastical court. After such a divorce, permission may be granted for a new marriage.[38]

However the natural solvent of the bond of marriage, of course, is death, after which the surviving partner may contract a second or, by special dispensation, even a third marriage.[39]

In the event of marital failure, the priest investigates the situation and submits a report to the ecclesiastical court, together with a statement on what he has done to aid the couple. In current practice, the courts deal pastorally with the couple, showing concern not only for the innocent spouse but also for the repentant one. The Orthodox have not remained unaffected by the changes through which churches and families have been moving in recent years. They, like the other denominations in this study, are attempting to meet the challenge within their tradition and their understanding of the Gospel.

Sectarian Groups

Protestantism by its very nature defies classification. In any typology of denominational lines, some churches will not fit. A selection of these independent, more sectarian bodies shows some consistency in standard and style.

Serious commitment to Jesus' words "Let no man put asunder" characterizes the Seventh Day Adventist attitude to indissolubility. For Adventists, our Lord had established a rule of conduct for the church under the dispensation of grace which must transcend forever all civil enactments that might go beyond this interpretation of the divine law regarding the marriage relationship.

In the event of marital strife, members are required to make an earnest endeavor to reconciliation, even where infidelity is the cause. In the event that reconciliation is not effected, the innocent spouse has the right to divorce and remarry. But the unrepentant guilty party is to be disfellowshiped. The guilty party has no right to remarry while the spouse remains unmarried and chaste. Should he do so, then disfellowshiping follows for both the separated spouse and the person he subsequently marries. Adventist ministers are prohibited from officiating at the weddings of any divorced persons except the innocent party in a case of adultery.

This same standard is reflected in the rule of The Jehovah's

Witnesses. Remarriage after divorce "without Scriptural permission or authorization is adulterous and the congregation will disfellowship the offender." [40] No member of the Witnesses may marry "a worldly person who was divorced on unscriptural grounds." To do so is interpreted as fornication, and the penalty is to be disfellowshiped.

In The Church of the Nazarene marriage is a binding, indissoluble covenant. Those who divorce under civil law where no scriptural grounds exist and who remarry are branded adulterous, no matter how justified under civil law. Their ministers are positively forbidden to conduct weddings of those not having scriptural grounds to wed.

The Christian and Missionary Alliance is on record as being unalterably opposed to divorce on any other than positive Scriptural grounds. Their ministers are forbidden to perform marriage ceremonies for divorced persons. And members who may have been divorced and consequently remarried (evidently in some extra church ceremony) cannot be elected or appointed to national offices in the church or given church credentials or Christian worker certificates.

The Advent Christian Church echoes disapproval of any and all divorces unscripturally obtained. Their ministers are forbidden to officiate at such remarriages.

The Reorganized Church of Christ, Latter Day Saints (not to be confused with the older body known as The Church of Jesus Christ, Latter Day Saints, referred to above) understands marriage to be indissoluble within the life-time of the spouses; in their doctrine, "the sacramental nature of marriage" requires that only those persons may wed one another who share this conviction and are willing to abide by its necessary conditions. The church recognizes that the remarriage of an innocent party in a divorce is permissible when the divorce was granted for adultery, repeated sexual perversion, or desertion. Ministers who officiate at such nuptials are advised to counsel carefully and to make sure that sufficient time has elapsed between marriages so that parties do not marry hastily.

The Protestant sects are marked by a larger emphasis upon discipline in this question of marriage as well as in other matters, as were the larger denominations some years ago.

The Baptists

Baptists, who make up the largest Protestant group in the U.S.A., are organized into free churches, each parish congregation being responsible for its own constitution and ordinances. Traditions of creed, canon law, or magisterium are foreign to their history. Nevertheless the major Baptist conventions of churches operate with a homogeneity and teach a basically similar doctrine. It is possible, therefore, to form approximate generalizations about their customary approach to the problem of marital indissolubility.

Baptist tradition views marriage as God-ordained and enduring until death. Divorce is acknowledged but recognized as a failure on the part of both husband and wife. As other denominations, the Baptists see their marriage and divorce practice in transition since the early 1960's. According to one spokesman [41] a new emphasis on forgiveness for marital failure has impressed The Southern Baptist Convention as it has other churches. Now it is possible to find church officers and some teachers among the divorced, a condition unthinkable some years ago. And there are, here and there, a few divorced ministers. A more understanding attitude to marriage failure has allowed some of these clergy to continue to serve as pastors, usually after moving to a new charge in another community.

Divorce and remarriage among Baptists are no longer treated as unpardonable sins, but the restrictions continue in many conservative parishes. Some pastors refuse absolutely to perform any weddings of previously married persons. Others will accept only the innocent partner from a union broken by adultery for consideration in weddings of the previously married. Still other pastors accept responsibility for remarriages according to the case; these tend to counsel carefully in the specific situation. And yet a fourth group evidently consider the marriage license itself as the sole qualification; reportedly they will bless the wedding of anyone.

The American Baptist Convention and The Disciples of Christ are two additional groups whose standards and current history are roughly parallel to this description of the Southern Baptists. But these bodies have moved in recent years to press for uniform marriage and divorce legislation throughout the nation in order to reduce abuses. Typical is a convention resolution from the Disciples in 1966 which requested the President of the United States to assemble a commission of citizens of special competence to draft an up-to-date, comprehensive, uniform code of laws concerning marriage and divorce and to suggest appropriate channels and measures for its implementation.

Pastoral theologians of the Baptist tradition have urged their ministers to marry only those previously wed persons who take seriously the claims of the faith regarding commitment and repentance and who will accept counseling. At the same time parish churches have begun to take a stand regarding marriage regulations, no longer leaving the decision solely to the pastor. All in all, Baptist bodies tend, as the statement from the Seventh Day Baptists phrases it, "to minister with special care and love to troubled persons."

Prevailing Directions

Among Protestant churches we have enjoyed a cheerful, Christian plagiarism for many years. Cooperative programs and ecumenical theology have long since produced a spate of statements and pronouncements that tend to look much alike. This same situation is evident in doctrine and pastoralia concerning Christian marriage.

We have seen, for example, that the majority of these

denominations have been moving away from legalistic standards, e.g., identifying a guilty party in marital failure, or considering adultery *per se* to be the worst or the only true marital offense. So, too, we have discovered over and again the Gospel emphases on reconciliation and forgiveness, opening the way for a new and Christian family founded in penitence for past sins and resolve for a holy marriage, even if that be a remarriage. Moreover we have noted the pervading influence of pastoral theology with its deep concern for persons and their family relationships as well as for church regulations; this has, admittedly, bent some laws in order to find saving grace for wounded men and women. The churches are in transition regarding their work with marriage.

Protestant bodies are sensitive to societal conditions and, as H. Richard Niebuhr saw, reveal social forces mediated through their tradition until the culture itself can be mistaken for the faith.[42] That this is likewise true for the Roman Catholic Church is obvious; yet it is the peculiar mark of Protestants. Will Herberg, author of *Protestant, Catholic, Jew,* once observed that as time goes on both Catholics and Jews in America tend more to resemble the Protestants, that is, they grow more secular.[43] And the secular environment makes its profound impact. In America, as Margaret Mead has noted, "marriage may be for life, can be for life, but also may not be. . . . [Divorce] may come to any marriage, no matter how devoted, how conscientious, how much in love each spouse originally was." [44] Yet to assume that God cannot be acting through our out-of-joint times is base unfaith. The secular, as many contemporary theologians have reminded us, is God's world, and his revelation can also be found in such an extra-ecclesiastical arena.

It is impossible to view this question of indissolubility only from the vantage of one church. Too many other churches and too many other forces profoundly affect our dogma, whether we admit them or not. There are at once marked similarities and vast differences between the Roman Catholic Church and Protestant churches regarding the ideal of indissolubility.

All of them have felt the effect of these cultural forces. They have together found themselves in historical transition, have puzzled over the growth of alternative family styles—of which divorce and remarriage is but one. Their divorce rates, we have seen, are more alike than different. Biblical theologians have pointed out to all churches where our over-simplified or culturally convenient interpretations of marriage and divorce lections may be suspect. We all know that also with the devout "it can even happen that a believer comes to the conclusion that his marriage does not bind him in conscience." [45]

On the other hand the dissimilarities are undeniable. Protestant churches lack any statement as majestic and formidable as Canon 1118: "Marriage which is *ratum et consummatum* cannot be dissolved by any human power, nor by any cause except death." Protestants have no obvious parallel to some of the provisos that follow in subsequent canons, e.g., 1119 through 1125, no dispensations "in favor of the faith," no legal machinery to handle "disparity of cult," the emphases on tests for consummation, or decision for a solemn religious profession, or the far-reaching effects of baptism in the consideration of marital cases: these are uniquely Catholic. A Presbyterian or Methodist may regard them with some dismay, even as do not a few Catholics today.

Clearly, then, our problem of marriage stability has patent ecumenical connotations. The recent studies that have brought us together for mutual work on the subject are to be encouraged, for this problem admits of no isolated denominational solution. The Baptists and the Disciples give us one clue in their clamor for a uniform national law on marriage and divorce. The Christian Family Movement shows us another as they welcome families of many persuasions into common endeavor in an apostolate to the home. Our newly revised approaches to pre-marital guidance, acknowledging that young couples require much the same help to begin marriage whether they are in St. Patrick's parish or Reformation Lutheran are to the point. As churches prayerfully restudy their canons, constitutions, resolutions, and regulations they will, in God's providence, find the way to speak anew the old word of his redemptive will to contemporary couples.

NOTES

1. Emil Brunner, *The Divine Imperative* (Philadelphia: Westminster Press, 1947), p. 362.
2. William J. Goode, *The Family* (Englewood Cliffs: Prentice-Hall, Inc., 1964), Ch. 9.
3. John Cuber, "An Alternative Model from the Perspective of Sociology," in *The Family in Search of a Future*, ed. Herbert Otto (New York: Appleton-Century-Crofts, 1970).
4. Alfred E. Kinsey, et al., *Sexual Behavior in the Human Female* (Philadelphia: W. B. Saunders, 1953), p. 11.
5. John A. Siramaki, *The American Family in the Twentieth Century* (Cambridge, Harvard University Press, 1953).
6. Wayne E. Oates, *Pastoral Counseling in Social Problems* (Philadelphia: Westminster Press, 1966), pp. 105, 107.
7. Rosemary Ruether, "Divorce: No Longer Unthinkable," in *Commonweal*, April 14, 1967, p. 118.
8. See William Barclay, *Commentary on Matthew*, Vol. I (Philadelphia: Westminster Press, 1958), pp. 148ff.; Helmut Thielicke, *The Ethics of Sex* (New York: Harper and Row, 1964), p. 183; Emil Brunner, *The Divine Imperative, op. cit.*, p. 351.
9. Rosemary Ruether, "Divorce: No Longer Unthinkable," *art. cit.*, p. 117.
10. Emil Brunner, *The Divine Imperative, op. cit.*, p. 354.
11. *The Westminster Confession of Faith* (Manchester: R. Aikman and Son, 1937), Ch. XXIV, Section V.
12. *Ibid.*, Ch. XXIV, Sections V and VI.
13. "The Directory for Worship," *The Constitution of the United Presbyterian Church in the U.S.A.* (Philadelphia: United Presbyterian Church in the U.S.A.), 22:01.
14. "The Book of Order Form of Government," *ibid.*, 42:28.
15. *Marriage, Divorce and Remarriage: A Commentary on the Westminster Confession of Faith* (Toronto: The Presbyterian Church of Canada, 1964), p. 16.
16. Karl Barth, *Church Dogmatics*, III/4 (Edinburgh: T. and T. Clark, 1961), p. 211.

17. *Minutes of The General Assembly* (Richmond: The Presbyterian Church of the United States, 1958).

18. *A Statement On Marriage and Divorce* (Toronto: The Presbyterian Church of Canada, 1972), p. 6.

19. "The Church and the Family," Resolution of the General Conference of the United Methodist Church, 1968.

20. "Statement of Social Principles," Section II, B. Resolution of the General Conference of the United Methodist Church, 1972.

21. William Graham Cole, "The Church and Divorce," in *Pastoral Psychology,* September, 1958.

22. A statement adopted at The General Convention of The American Lutheran Church, 1956.

23. Bernard Häring, *Shalom: The Sacrament of Reconciliation* (New York: Doubleday Image Books, 1969), pp. 308f.

24. "Sex, Marriage and Family" adopted by the Fifth Biennial Convention, 1970, The Lutheran Church in America.

25. H. G. Coiner, "Those 'Divorce and Remarriage' Passages," in *The Concordia Theological Monthly,* June 1968, p. 381. Italics mine.

26. A statement adopted at The General Convention of The American Lutheran Church, 1964.

27. Carl F. Reuss, "Marriage, Divorce, and Remarriage," in *Helping Families Through the Church,* revised, ed. Oscar E. Feucht (St. Louis: Concordia Publishing House, 1971), p. 238.

28. "Sex, Marriage and Family," *art. cit.*

29. Helmut Thielicke, *The Ethics of Sex, op. cit.,* p. 164.

30. Günter Bornkamm, "Die Stellung des NT Z. Ehescheidung, Ein Gutachten," in *Evangelischen, Theologie,* 1948, 9/10, p. 284.

31. Carl F. Reuss in *Helping Families Through the Church, op. cit.,* p. 242.

32. From *The Lambeth Conference, 1867-1948* (London: S.P.C.K., 1948).

33. "Marriage and Family Life, Part IV (Toronto: The Anglican Church of Canada, undated), p. 34.

34. Derrick Sherwin Bailey, *The Mystery of Love and Marriage* (New York: Harper and Bros., 1952), pp. 74-95.

35. *Ibid.,* p. 78.

36. John A. T. Robinson, *Honest To God* (Philadelphia: Westminster Press, 1963), p. 111.

37. On this point Frank Gavin quotes Constantine Dyobouniotes, *Ta Musteria Tes Anatolikes Orthodoxou Ekklesias ex Epopseus Dogmatikes* (Athens, 1912), in his own *Greek Orthodox Thought* (Milwaukee, 1923), p. 380.

38. I. E. Mesolora, *Symbolike Tes Orthodoxou Anatolikes Ekklesias* (Athens: The Church of Greece, 1883), Vol. I, p. 351.

39. Christos Androutsos, *Dogmatike Tes Orthodoxou Anatolikes Ekklesias* (Athens: Astir, 1956), p. 399.

40. *The Watchtower,* October 1, 1956, p. 597.

41. The Rev. Herman Green, Jr., family life consultant, The Southern Baptist Convention.

42. H. Richard Neibuhr, *Christ and Culture* (New York: Harper and Bros., 1951), pp. 83-115.

43. Will Herberg, *Protestant, Catholic, Jew* (New York: Doubleday and Co., 1955).

44. Margaret Mead, *Male and Female* (New York: W. Morrow, 1949), p. 357.

45. *The Dutch Catechism* as quoted in *Herder Correspondence*, January, 1967.

Helen McDaniel

A Social Agency
Looks at the Family

"The principal cause of marriage
failure is the great expectation
that most people have." "All
marriages are in an equilibrium state; if the balance shifts,
there is trouble." "The liberation of women is causing the
shift in roles. Some people can't adjust." "Many people
have not achieved maturity, so they're not ready for inter-
dependence." "Most couples today do not enter marriage with
the respect they used to have for the binding nature of
marriage."

These were comments from a group of social workers who
are presently engaged in family and marriage counseling. They
went on to say, "Many people are ignorant of what the
Church really teaches about marriage." "Mobility, lack of
therapeutic family relationships, etc., have had their effect
upon marriage stability." "A lot of young people are weigh-
ing what they want out of marriage and not rushing into it
out of dependency."

There are social service agencies under the sponsorship of
the Catholic Church in most of the dioceses. These agencies
were started primarily as a supplemental service to institutions. After the large waves of immigration, children's homes,
unmarried mothers' homes, etc., were built to answer the
needs of the people. They were a means to protect the faith
of the Catholic people. The agencies were started to provide
counseling as a prerequisite to placement of children. Family

89

and marriage counseling for many of these agencies is relatively new. As a matter of fact, counseling itself grew rapidly in all social service agencies after the great impact of psychotherapy on social work. The 1960's brought a new dimension of systems analyses and the new theories of learning, communication, etc. The 1960's also brought new threats to the family.

The Church agency has traditionally been viewed as an arm of the Church to carry out its mission to care for the homeless, the widowed, the orphaned, etc. All of the major religions have some form of social service as a commitment. The social service agency found itself with a mandate to be an arm of the Church in these matters. At the same time, it competed for Church funds to carry out these objectives. As the social service worker became more professionalized, he became involved in therapy and tended to neglect the preventive and social action aspects of family life. Many dioceses added Family Life Bureaus for this task. The social service agency on many occasions received referrals for families after the parish priest had done his best to keep a couple together or to keep children from being placed. Many of the agencies also have become financed through a variety of means—by the Church, by fees for services, by community funds and/or by a government subsidy. Many of the agencies started by Protestant denominations have become community agencies. Most of the Catholic and Jewish agencies have very strong ties with their sponsors, although they may have multiple resources for funding. In a recent survey of the pastors in the Columbus diocese, we found that nearly half of them were not aware that Catholic Social Service did Family and Marriage Counseling.

The Marriage or Diocesan Tribunal in Columbus was set apart from the Church-sponsored social service agency because it is judicatory in function. Much of their work has carried an aura of legalism which was highly secretive and terribly important. How decisions were made was a mysterious process and, as far as the average layman was concerned, affected only the relationship of those involved. The timing was completely out of step with cases which were known to the social service agency. Although the two agencies were in the same building, we seldom, if ever, worked with the same clients at the same time. There were few, if any, referrals between the two agencies. In recent years this has begun to change. In our diocese we are now being asked to make assessments of a person's ability to formulate a relationship. Some dioceses have been asked to offer counsel and give assessments of relationships between young people (below 18 years of age) who are asking permission to marry because of pregnancy.

Traditionally, the American family has imitated its predecessor in Europe. Its history goes back into early times, prior to the birth of Christ. As an institution it has been tough. It has survived wars, fates of environmental disasters, revolutions, both political and cultural, but as in all periods of trials and tribulations, the present-day problems seem to be the greatest. Only history can testify as to the truth of this assumption. At any rate, it would seem that there is more disruption in the structure of the family now than any other time known to us. The traditional nuclear family with two parents, grandparents, 3.5 children and a kin network seems to be giving way to some emerging family types. The commune, the unmarried parent-child family, the two adults of the same sex and adopted child are all types of families which seem to threaten our whole value system which has been transmitted through the traditional family structure.[1]

The fate of the family cannot be divorced from other factors which are present in our culture. Pressures from inside the family and outside seem to be bending it and straining it beyond endurance. "Will it survive?" we ask ourselves. Based upon years of suffering through good times and bad, it is difficult to know which work more unfavorably for the family. If it is the most natural habitat for security from outside dangers, then one might predict that natural disasters, hard times, etc., should force the family to be more dependent upon its members. This kind of intimacy should make it grow as an institution. On the other hand, if there are disruptions within the social order, it may result in differences of opinions which would divide the family as a unit. Perhaps the conditions are present today which cause disruptions both within and outside the system.

Another possibility is that the family has tended to be a safeguard for passing on values which are being tested and found wanting in our culture. Some of the myths that we have tended to cling to are: All men are created equal; there is a new frontier and opportunity is ever present; man can overcome his environment; criticism of any feature of any system is being disloyal. As young people began to question some of the operations of the family as well as the Church, it seemed that they were disloyal and the stresses and strains have become hard for parents to cope with. Also advanced knowledge about the reproductive system and certain cultural changes about child care have tended to release many women from child-bearing and also child-rearing responsibilities. The influence of the ever present television has also helped us to shape expectations which may never be met. At any rate it has offered many an otherwise inter-dependent family to escape necessary communication.

As marriage and family counselors, we have achieved much of our knowledge about marriage through divorce. We look at what went wrong. We tend to tabulate the inter-relationship factors which are not meeting the mutual needs of the partners. We see inter-relatedness between the love two parents have for one another and their ability to love their children. We see relatedness between the parents' ability to cope with frustrations and their ability to teach their children how to cope. We see relatedness between a parent's ability to formulate relationships on the job and within the home. Sometimes people cope by forming defenses to tolerate a situation. Counselors are trained to recognize these and help to modify those defenses which are unhealthy.

Divorce was an indication in the past that there had been failure. Some people may not blame themselves for a divorce but tend to accept it as a societal norm. The attitudes of Church people are not *too* different from those of the rest of society. For example, many attitudes have tended to change long before the institutional Church has accepted them as changes. We suspect, though, that many marriages are failing today which would have made it in the past. Some would have worked out their problems and others would have continued to suffer, preferring that to divorce.

The changing pattern of the roles between men and women has left some persons in confusion and some marital pairs unstable. We have tended to depend almost exclusively on the apprentice system for learning about marriage. Couples today are the same people whose models have not necessarily coped with present-day problems. For example, women have not in all cultures, been the child-rearer, yet in our culture, up until the present generation, they have been expected to be. Although a mother may have worked in an office, a factory or a professional setting, she was still responsible for the rearing of her child. If anything went wrong, she was to blame. Although she may have worked outside the home, she was still responsible for it to be run without confusion, hire an acceptable baby-sitter and be available for all that needed to be done for the children. She also had to nurse the husband back to health.

Many women are beginning to question that role and are being quite noisy about it. When we speak of other liberation movements, we are speaking of minorities as a rule. Women's liberation has the best opportunity of succeeding. With its success, however, it brings more confusion about roles than any of the other movements. The "mystique" of motherhood is no longer the only model for a woman. No longer does she seem to be a failure if she has neither married nor borne a child. Couples have begun to see other tests of fullness of life than the ability to conceive, bear and rear children.

The confusion which we have observed in marriage counseling has come largely from the husband. The husband who learned about the role of the father from his father and mother finds himself without a model. The wife often gravitates to the new role with a feeling of freedom. The pent-up resentment of having to be all things to her husband and children can now be verbalized without a feeling of guilt. Husbands are normally torn apart with this attitude which was relatively unexpected. Coping with it sometimes destroys his self-image of masculinity. This is further complicated by competition he may experience at work.

We know that, in the past, displacement of feelings has often occurred either at the home or at the office. Man in particular had the two environments to play against one another. This now becomes a problem when he may not be the master in either environment.

It would be a mistake to point to this liberation movement as only a problem for men. Women, while enjoying it, may find themselves in a position of confusion. Their former defenses which were attributed to women cannot be used. They are often accused of wanting both worlds. They, too, may over-react to the new freedom and find they are missing some of the secondary benefits of being dependent creatures. This all calls for new maturity in marriages and man-wife relationships. The balance of inter-dependence does not come as naturally as some would desire.

Those of us who are in the helping professions find ourselves in need of further training for the tasks which are presented. Most of us are used to helping couples achieve stability through counseling based upon insight into the results of certain choices. Counseling of married couples who are seeking adjustment in the past has usually consisted of helping people listen to one another, offering alternatives which would help in the making of choices and supporting the persons in those decisions which seemed right for them. Suddenly we find ourselves in a new ball game. Certain behavior may no longer result in isolation. Community norms are changing. For example, it may be possible today to enter the "gay" world and not be chastised. There is an open-endedness about values which is unsettling even to the counselors.

We begin to question our practice and find that past experience does not necessarily help to foretell the future.

With all of these difficulties, there is still a ring of honesty in approaching the future which is somewhat more encouraging than in the past. I can remember an older counselor once stating that some marriages stand a better chance of survival if there are extra-marital affairs. This seems to be a rather shaky state of affairs. Alcoholism, mental illness and the whole battery of escape practices would seem to be more necessary in this kind of make-believe world.

The question might be for the future, "Can we stand all of the honesty and realism that we are bargaining for?" Dr. Brissenden, a psychiatrist who taught at O.S.U. School of Social Work, said in 1963: "Our generation produced the neurotics who knew right from wrong, did what was wrong and then suffered untold guilt about it. This generation is producing the character disorders who don't know right from wrong so they don't feel guilty." [2] Guilt is the great motivator for avoiding wrong-doing.

Marriage in the past has often involved a closed mate selection process. With the mobility of youth this has changed considerably in recent years. Co-habitation patterns have changed in the past five years. Colleges are moving from the *loco parentis* role. All of these opportunities for young people to formulate relationships which produce intimacy very quickly will have their effect upon the future of the family. At this time, we cannot predict what specific effect will emerge. We do know that counseling cannot be an advice-giving process that many supposed it should be in the past. Our future case-load will be comprised of persons whose life-experiences will far exceed those of the counselors.

The Church as a Community

"The Christian community is truly a sacrament. Its work is essentially unitive because it gives witness to the solidarity of mankind. As servant or served, the individual Christian is living proof that all is done in the name of Jesus as brother to another. . . ." [3] The Church has tended to de-emphasize its various social ministries and has not viewed them as part of its sacramental system. Theologians like Richard McBrien have advocated new thoughts on this matter. He suggests: "The Church is the community of those who confess the lordship of Jesus Christ, who ratify that faith in baptism and who thereby commit themselves to membership and mission within that sacramental community of faith. But the primary reality is the kingdom of God, and the existence and function of the Church make no sense apart from it. The mission is threefold in relationship to the reign of God: to proclaim in word and sacrament the definitive arrival of the kingdom of Jesus in Nazareth (kerygma), to offer itself as a test case of its own proclamation, as a group transformed by the Spirit into a community of faith, hope, love, and truthfulness—a sign of the kingdom on earth and an anticipation of the kingdom of the future (koinonia), and finally to realize and extend the reign of God through service in the socio-political order (diakonia)." [4]

Recently the National Conference of Catholic Charities has undergone a self-study. The report of the first phase of the study is at the present time being reviewed by the membership. This report, after a year of deliberations, makes suggestions about the unity of programs of the Church which would tend to be a witness of Christ's love for people. Too often the various Church programs have been isolated and seen as units in themselves. Too often they have relieved the individual of his responsibility to perform acts of charity and justice.

Most dioceses have the following programs which are concerned with the family as a unit: the educational system, the family life bureau, the charities programs and the diocesan tribunal all are interested in both preventive and curative programs for the family. On a diocesan basis these systems could quite feasibly work more effectively together. Unfortunately, they have to compete for the same funds and the same human resources in carrying out their individual mandates. At the very minimum they could work together toward unified approaches and coordinated activities.

The wealth of knowledge in all of these individual offices could well be used for helping each program in its effectiveness.

New Life Styles

Many young people are testing personal and sexual compatibility before marriage. Co-habitation in college, living together, traveling on extensive vacations, etc., are bringing about life experiences which have both benefits and problems. Dorothy Fahs Beck of the Family Service Association of America outlined these in a recent presentation. Based on a study at Cornell University, the benefits for some were (1) better understanding of self, and (2) promotion of growth and maturity. The problems which were experienced were (1) pervasive sexual problems, (2) frequent abortions and unwanted pregnancies, (3) parental disapproval and concealment from parents, (4) delay in identity developments due to over-involvement in relationships, (5) lack of privacy, and (6) feelings of guilt.

Not only experiences prior to marriage are having an effect upon the family but other trends are appearing after marriage. Condominiums, full-life planned apartment villages, small neighborhood gatherings, group security communes, etc., are changing the life style of many young married couples. These, too, are offering opportunities for quickly formed relationships. It is easy to formulate benefits and problems which may emerge from these styles. Some benefits would be (1) accessible companionship, (2) mutual aid in solving emergencies, (3) available help in case of sickness, etc. Many of the expectations of true neighbors may be fulfilled. Some of the problems would be (1) lack of privacy, (2) surface relationships which may not hold up under critical times, (3) lack of space for a growing family, and (4) unwanted pregnancies.

Changing Mores

Sexual mores are discussed more openly now than in any time we can recall. There is increased pressure to remove legal controls on sexual practices between consenting adults. There are changing standards on pornography and obscene literature.

Social workers and other professionals are in the middle of a controversy. The National Association of Social Workers at its Delegate Assembly (1971) voted to go on record in favor of liberalized abortion laws. Its reasons were: (1) the child is not a human person until it is born and therefore has no rights; (2) the expectant mother has a right to make a decision as to whether or not to continue a pregnancy; (3) abortions will continue outside the legal structure if the laws are not changed, and this will lead to dangerous operations; (4) population must be controlled or the quality of life is threatened. Many proponents see the person who goes on record against such liberalization as imposing his mores upon the rest of society. There is presently a movement within the profession of social work to force all social workers to inform the client of the availability of pro-abortion counseling.

All of these changing mores will have their effect upon the stability of marriage. For example, we may well assume that premarital sexual acts will become more prevalent. The tendency for persons to decide for themselves as to the appropriateness of their behavior changes the role of the counselor. At this point, we do not clearly see the extent of this change. Some of the possibilities are: (1) Without guilt, the anxiety for change will be weakened; without anxiety, counseling has little with which to work. (2) If the tendency will be to create lasting values and more sensitivity toward people, the counselor then may be of help in the following ways: (a) providing leadership in creating situations in which the individual may test his stated values as to their credibility; (b) providing group sessions through which communications can be clear and articulated; (c) providing more preventative sessions which would better prepare people to enter into marriage with values which are shared and lasting; (d) working with others who are attempting to work toward stabilizing the marriage bond and the family.

We should not assume that people wish to enter into a valueless society. Most people realize that this would result in chaos and offer little security for anyone. Perhaps the best approach would be to seek out the objectives young people have, give them an opportunity to articulate their values and also help them to test their validity. For young married couples, we may well ask them to participate in formulating policy with which they will have to live. The preamble of the recent study of the National Conference of Catholic Charities states: "Programs benefit people only when they contribute to the individual's freedom and independence. Catholic Charities must commit itself boldly to the liberation of man so that he can be the real artisan of his destiny, the shaper of history, the free builder of his future." [5]

The Church must re-establish its credibility with people. The renewal of the structure, liturgy and programs demonstrates that it is in this process. There is some danger that it is not talking to all of its constituency. How to do this is an obstacle for many who are not used to reaching out to listen. We must continually ask ourselves how would Christ do it. Depending on who asks the question, the answer will vary. On the other hand, maybe we should ask this of the various persons who are in leadership positions. We also should review our programs to see if they are the ones which are most needed today. In doing this we should look at the Church programs and place priorities on our expenditures.

These priorities should in some way be placed according to an objective need. Whitney Young once said, "Programs don't have to be eternal to become immortal."

Rather than delegate certain aspects of life to the different agencies of the Church, a coordinated and cooperative plan for the enrichment of all life should be developed. We should expect that group living will continue in some form or other, and as far as we know the family plan is the one which will survive. Its stability will rest upon the stability of our culture and the ability to achieve appropriate norms and values which are operational and practical.

Within our culture there are many marriages which are surviving the turbulence which has been noted over and over again. We should devote some human and financial resources to finding out why this is so. Rather than depend upon pathology for our knowledge, let us turn to health and study it objectively. Such research could be embarked upon in a collaborative style. One discipline alone may not be able to design an effective study.

When we speak of healthy marriages, we don't necessarily suggest that there are marriages which are blissfully happy. Certain symptoms which we would look for are: mutual satisfaction in the way most crises are met; open communication which allows for expression of ideas and plans; few secrets except those which tend to preserve some privacy; a feeling of growth, wonderment and celebration; and a deep respect for one another. Sadness, disappointments, discovery of faults and the like are part of living. These do not ruin a marriage but tend to strengthen it when approached with charity and maturity.

There are marriages which survive but in which people are hurting one another and also, many times, the children. Helping these families to define their needs and building programs to strengthen these limping-along families would be a true asset to people. Most of our programs in family life education do not meet the needs of such families. How to make these programs attractive and relevant to the real needs of people must be worked upon by a team of people with advice from those to be served.

Other Factors

Many environmental circumstances are irritants to stable family life. For the poor and marginal income family, we need to develop concern, not just official concern but the concern of the Christian family collectively. There are many attitudes which are prevalent today that are basically destructive to other individuals. We need to develop advocacy programs for these people. There are myths continuing to operate which are not only destructive to the victims of such discrimination but are destructive to those who fail to correct the injustices. Most of the liberation movements are indicative of past discriminations which locked people into prisons of one type or another. True liberation will happen when all people are treated with respect and have an opportunity to achieve maturity and their God-given potential. Liberation for groups to practice self-harm and harm to others, of course, will have to be curtailed as in any civilized society, but some of our laws which militate against justice and keep others restricted from enjoying the fruits of our land need to be changed. On the other hand, some people are protected by law but not in fact.

Many of our people are living in alienated surroundings because of our secular society. We realize that social workers have been asked to do for people many of the things that neighbors once did for each other. We must in some way reverse this trend. For one thing, we can't afford it; for another, it ruins the basic Christian community. Social work can provide programs for people and offer expertise which the ordinary person cannot provide. When it takes away from the individual the opportunity to practice personal Christian charity, it does an injustice to all.

Summary

The Church, as a community, offers an opportunity to worship, to serve and be served, to teach and to be a witness of its founder. In the past we have seen a hierarchy of values which relegated services to the last place. This was not done in conscience, as service has continued to be emphasized in sermons and in some practical way by the building of institutions. However, the social ministry was not seen as a sacrament. The sacrifice and the teaching of the Church have been given priority in terms of human and financial resources.

We are suggesting that equal importance be given to the social ministries of the Church. Religion does not operate in a vacuum. It has always served a very functional role in any society. When it does not meet the needs of society, the institutional form has often changed. This should not be necessary if we see the Church as a community and allow it to adapt to the needs of people. This would not alter its basic beliefs but would enhance its meaning to people.

Any society needs a value system and a code of ethics which tells us how to live with one another. We are beginning to see that some of the values which Church people have are not necessarily essential to the dictates of the religion they practice. Separating cultural factors and religious factors is not as easy as one would like to believe. Vatican II has shown us this. Renewal in Catholicism has meant getting rid of or shedding some of the practices which were not essential to its existence. With this has come a renewal of the sensitivity toward the needs of people.

The breaking down of norms which have been a support to us in the past, has led many to fear complete chaos and anomie. This should not necessarily be the case. Every institution has suffered from tension. This may be necessary for the creation of enough anxiety to change. If we are completely honest, we must recognize that many people suffered injustices under the past regimes. Perhaps the future will be brighter for all. We know that as long as some are suffering, we are all suffering.

The family as the basic unit of society has probably felt the tensions, stresses and change more than any institution to which we belong. It has been the cradle of our value system and has reinforced all of the other attitudes we have felt to be important. When it begins to weaken, we all feel threatened. The evidence seems to be that the family as we have known it is changing.

Sometimes we are guilty of being prophets of gloom and show no faith, although we profess to having faith every time we recite the Creed. As in all changes in history, there have been people who have observed the changes, analyzed them for what they are, recognized the good and made recommendations for adaptation for the future.

Should we look at the past 500 years, we can recognize some of our errors and how this has caused others to suffer. We must realize that the values we have taught our children have crystallized many injustices to others. Maybe the family reaction to the present crises is a healthy reaction to some false values and myths which should not be retained. The real problem will be how to pull out of this present chaos the values which truly represent Christ. How will we institutionalize these for the future generations?

Human services must take their place in the Christianity of the future. This makes the Church credible. Social service must work hand in hand with social advocacy and religious education. It must not be practiced by a few or relegated to an agency. Somehow, all of God's people must be both server and served.

The family, the marriage and the relationship of the family to its environment should be the target of all of the agencies of the Church. Inter-disciplinary seminars should be of help in planning for the future. Too often programs are fragmented and self-praising. If the Church is to become a community, its people must work for it to do so.

NOTES

1. Alvin Toffler, *Future Shock* (New York: Random House, 1970), pp. 211-230.
2. Unpublished notes from class at Ohio State University, 1963.
3. Unpublished self-study, *National Conference of Catholic Charities,* Washington, D.C., 1972.
4. Rev. Richard McBrien, *Catholic Charities, Why and Whither,* Lecture at National Conference of Catholic Charities, Minneapolis, Minn., 1971.
5. Self-study, *op. cit.*

Andrew M. Greeley

Church Marriage Procedures and the Contemporary Family

Before one can make any useful comments from the sociological perspective on the contemporary family, one must clear away a good deal of nonsense that poses as sociology in the mass media or in the pseudo-elite journals, such as *The Saturday Review* and *The New York Review of Books*. If one obtains one's view of social reality from such literature (and a considerable number of Americans, especially American clergy, do), one would think that the family is "falling apart," and that "swinging" (as spouse-swapping is currently called), pre-marital and extra-marital sex, group orgies, communal sex, and perhaps even forms of polygamy and polyandry are replacing the traditional nuclear family. The wise men who fabricate articles for such journals nod their heads solemnly and say that "new forms" of family life are emerging.

None of this phony wisdom ought to be taken seriously. The overwhelming majority of Americans do not engage in most of the behaviors that are supposed to be the wave of the future. Indeed, the behaviors themselves are all very ancient. The assumption that there is more infidelity or more pre-marital sex now than there has been at some unspecified age in the past is both undocumented and, from what we know of the past, simply not true. Furthermore, and most critically, the important thing to be said about the family is not that it is about to go out of business but rather that it is more important than ever before, that more emotional resources and energies are poured into the family relationship than in any previous time in human history. The real problem is not that the family is not important enough to typical Americans; it may be that the family is altogether too important.

It is certainly true that the family does not play the economic role in society that it used to play. It is no longer the basic unit of production, and after the early years of life (when all the really important work has been done), it is no longer the basic unit of education. But, as Professor Talcott Parsons has pointed out, having lost most of these secondary roles, the family now puts virtually all its emphasis on what is its primary function, human relationships. In the Western world (and in the industrial cities of the non-Western world where the middle-class family seems to be becoming dominant) and in the United States particularly, the family has become the principal and to a considerable extent the only source of emotional satisfaction and self-fulfillment available to modern man. Much more is expected from the marriage relationship than ever before in human history. The expectations and aspirations of a man and woman of their family life are incredibly high. Most college graduates, in fact, will say that they expect their principal satisfactions to come from the family, something which in all likelihood would never have been said before in human history.

In earlier eras it was required of a woman that she bring children into the world, see that they were properly dressed and fed, make sure that the house was neat and clean, and perhaps tend the garden and the chicken yard. The tasks were clearly specified, the means for executing them readily available, and the standards by which the performance was judged were clear and precise.

In contemporary American middle-class society, however, a woman is expected to be a chauffeur, a social planner, an educator, a therapist, a bookkeeper, and a mistress in addition to making sure that all the old housewifery chores are executed. Also, if she is at all in tune with the times, she knows that she is expected not only to give but to get sexual satisfaction as well as to demand a place for herself in the world of career and profession.

The man, on the other hand, is expected not only to fulfill the traditional roles of begetter and provider; he must also now contribute to the education of the children and to the social life of the community in which he lives. He must preside over (but only as the *primus inter pares*) the decision-making in a democratic family. He must be adept at switching from the style of the aggressive, competitive, hard-driving business or professional man to the tender, affectionate, supportive lover of his wife and children. Finally, more recently he is also expected to provide sexual satisfaction for his wife —an area in which he frequently feels both inadequate and incompetent, as the increased number of cases of impotency reported by psychiatrists seem to attest.

Instead of being a clearly specified set of contractual obligations in which both sides give and receive according to traditional norms, American marriage has become an experience, an encounter, a situation in which all parties are expected to "be themselves," to be "open, honest, and trusting," to risk themselves in "vulnerability." Marriage is an "I-thou" relationship into which both partners come with very high levels of expectation about the physical and emotional satisfactions they will obtain through interpersonal intimacy. Neither the man nor the woman may be skilled at intimacy, and neither is likely to have the kind of self-confidence and trust that is required for the risk-taking and vulnerability that intimacy demands, but American culture nonetheless requires that they expect tremendous payoff from it. The society has insisted that man and wife have fantastically high aspirations about the satisfactions to be obtained from marriage, but it has neglected to equip them with the skills and the self-esteem required to practice intimacy.

Some sociologists studying developing countries report that it is much easier for women there to move into the world of career precisely because these women expect much less from the marriage relationship than do American women. It is not that in such countries the marriage relationship is unimportant, but rather that it is not all-important. Paradoxically enough, because it is not all-important, these observers think that much higher levels of satisfaction are obtained in fact than in the United States where the expectations of satisfaction are much higher. The lower the level of expectation, in other words, the higher the level of achievement, not only in proportionate but perhaps even in absolute terms.

The principal crisis, then, in the American family comes not so much from the fact that the family is going out of fashion as from the fact that Americans have such great expectations for the happiness to be achieved in marriage. American culture seems to demand intimacy in the marriage relationship for which husbands and wives are but ill-prepared. "Swinging" among suburban couples is seen from such a perspective as an attempt to create the excitement and variety in sexual activity that was expected to come from the marriage relationship. The advocates of "swinging" argue frequently, almost in these very terms, that the release of sexual tension that results from spouse-swapping or from periodic group orgies actually improves the quality of the relationship between husband and wife. There may be a good deal of truth in this argument, but "swinging" is obviously an activity fraught with grave psychological dangers—not to say moral repulsiveness. It is nonetheless evidence of our level of expectation from marriage and the discouragement, frustration, and strain that results from the lack of capacity to live up to these expectations.

The quest for interpersonal intimacy and vulnerability, for openness and trust, surely must be positively received by those who are part of the Christian tradition. The problem is not that vulnerability in intimate relationships is not good; rather the problem is that married couples think that it is easily achieved, and so they enter marriage without the skills required to achieve it. Nor is there any provision made for helping them to develop such skills as the marriage relationship continues.

If there is to be any contribution at all from the Church to sustain a man and woman in marriage, it seems to me that it ought to be of the sort which helps them to acquire the confidence and the skills—and the realism—they need in their search for interpersonal vulnerability. Paradoxically, it seems that many of the more "radical" priests and marriage counselors think that their basic task is to justify pre-marital intercourse, when in fact it would seem that their most important contribution would be to support, reinforce, and sustain fidelity, which is herein defined as a constant mutual effort to enrich and develop a complex, demanding, wearying, and rewarding human relationship. (Note that "fidelity" is not defined as "the absence of infidelity." It is strange how we often define a highly positive quality in terms of "not doing" certain things. The basic instincts of the old Cana conferences were quite sound, although both the problems in marriage and the skills needed to overcome these problems were greatly underestimated by the original Cana theory and are misunderstood by many of the shallow modern "encounter" versions of Cana.)

If the principal problem of modern marriage is that the expectations for it may be unrealistically high and the skills with which it is approached tragically underdeveloped, what can one say of the Church's apparatus of matrimonial laws and tribunals?

The first observation is that they are, generally speaking, quite irrelevant to the problem under discussion. One would be hard put to make a case that the matrimonial legislation and procedures of the Church increase interpersonal problems in American marriage. But neither does the substantial investment of time, energy, and resources in the matrimonial apparatus make any positive contribution to improving the quality of married life among American Catholics. The matrimonial tribunals came into being in an era when none of the problems described in the previous paragraphs of this paper were operative. They were designed for a different world, and have very little to offer to the problems of the present.

The Church's marriage legislation came into being when marriage was primarily, if not exclusively, a contract concerned basically with the transmission and inheritance of property. Marriage today is much less a contract (though there is still in civil law contractual components) than an interpersonal commitment. It is much less concerned with the transmission of property than with the development of skills and experience in intimacy. It is probably inevitable and necessary that civil law change only very gradually in response to this new perspective on marriage (a perspective that, since it emphasizes commitment, responsibility, fidelity, intimacy, and love, ought to be applauded by everyone in the Christian tradition). What is most unfortunate is that ecclesiastical law—supposedly some sort of manifestation of religious wisdom—changes much more slowly, if at all, than civil law. From the religious viewpoint, interpersonal commitment is surely superior to legal contract. The giving of a gift to each other in full confidence of God's saving love ought to be much more admirable from the Christian viewpoint than the enforcement of a contract under provisions not unlike that required by Roman law. Not only is the Church's matrimonial apparatus irrelevant, it is also very likely a sign of a failure to recognize a critically important religious insight.

Therefore, the sociologist must address a certain number of questions to both the canon lawyers and the theologians who are concerned with the continuation of the matrimonial tribunals:

1. Is the definition of marriage as a contract part of the

essence of Christianity? Is it religiously impossible for us to accept the changing view of marriage from a contract to an interpersonal commitment?

2. Are those who are capable of entering into a legal contract necessarily capable of entering the kind of definitive personal commitment marriage is presently considered to be by most Americans? Is a marriage union permanent before a certain level of vulnerability and interpersonal unity is reached? Does marriage in fact become indissoluble at the moment it is physically consummated, or does it become indissoluble at some later point when the exchange of gift of personhood can, indeed, be said to have taken place?

3. Are marriage laws and the accompanying courts essential to the mission of the Church? Are they required either by the Gospel or by the tradition of the early Church? To what extent are they the result of social and cultural situations, which indeed once required that Church law supplement if not supplant civil marriage laws? Is it not possible that the social and cultural situations have changed so extensively that the Church ought to get out of the matrimonial law business and concentrate rather on religious ideals—an area in which it unquestionably has competence—and leave marital legis-lation to civil society?

4. Might a rather different approach to marriage be more effective? Do not the legislation and the matrimonial courts stand in the way of a different approach? Might not the appropriate course for the Church be to get out of the legal approach to marriage and invest all its resources in preaching religious ideals and in sustaining those couples who are seri-ously committed to living such ideals?

5. Is permanence in marriage a legal obligation that the Church is most likely to achieve through a complex system of laws and penalties, or is it a religious ideal that the Church is most likely to sustain by preaching the Gospel and providing social and religious support for married couples?

6. Finally, how long will the present system continue to be taken seriously by lower clergy and laity in the Church? The

data from the NORC study on the priests in the United States indicate that a substantial number of priests (and a majority of those under thirty-five) do not hesitate to give communion to those who have "divorced and remarried." It is an open secret that many priests have become their own matrimonial tribunals and make their own decisions at the parochial level without referring them to the diocesan tribunal. Does anyone seriously think that this tendency can be reversed? Are not the days of the matrimonial tribunals numbered in any event? And if attempts are made to keep them alive, will they not persist merely as hollow shells, to which recourse will be had only by the most tradition-bound priests and lay people? What will happen when lay people discover—
—as one presumes they are already discovering—that while a priest in one parish will require them to go to the tribunal, a priest in a neighboring parish will "dispense" from the necessity of going to the tribunal? Are not the days of the tribunal, in fact, numbered, and isn't that number rather small?

The import of all these questions is to suggest that the matrimonial tribunals and the legal structures that support them are relics of another age. Useful and valid in their own time, no doubt, they were neither part of the essence of Christianity nor are they especially pertinent now. The tribunals are in all likelihood part of the useless baggage we have carried from the past which ought to be discarded as soon as possible. They do not, I think, do a great deal of harm save to some of the people who get involved with them directly, and they will cause even less harm as years go by, because in a very short time practically no one will take them seriously. The real misfortune is that so much time, energy, resources, and attention is still expended on the courts that could be used to developing forms of witness-bearing for married couples that would be pertinent to the situations in which they find themselves.

One must ask, for example, whether the appropriate reaction for a Church that bears the Good News of God's loving mercy as manifested in Jesus Christ should be, when faced with an agonizing problem of impotence, to immediately proceed to determine whether the hymen has been perforated. Obviously, such behavior is ludicrous, disgraceful, and false to the genius of Christianity. How we became involved in such behavior is a question well worth asking, but even more important, we should ask how can we most quickly get out of such behavior and, indeed, out of the whole outmoded, irrelevant, stupid, and disgraceful apparatus.

Kevin Hern

A Positive
Approach From
Civil Law

There is need for more active participation by professionally qualified representatives of the Roman Catholic Church in the United States to meet and resolve the many marital problems of Catholics that tend more and more to end in the divorce courts. Yet, we know of few organizations within the Church structure designed for the specific purpose of supporting or rehabilitating marriages in the United States. Nor is there an adequate number of individuals or groups presented by the Church as trained and skilled in relevant areas to advise parties to a troubled marriage, certainly on a long-term basis.

Significant help could be given by the Church to many who seek a solution to marriage problems and the preservation of their homes. The well-intentioned advice and encouragement of the parish priest often is not enough, and in many instances people are unwilling to bring their difficulties to his attention.

The unavailability of a Catholic service of this importance means that marriages which could be saved deteriorate, and the partners and—more important—the children suffer irretrievable damage. Divorce then is too frequently the result.

The professional "marriage counselor" or the psychiatrist often is no adequate substitute. Relatively few apply to these problems the Catholic values essential to their understanding, and too many seem willing to recommend a permanent termination of the relationship without a thorough exploration of all relevant factors. The lawyer is not trained in long-term guidance. His attempts to achieve reconciliation often fail because of his inability to go to the root of the issue and because he is normally consulted by only one of the two parties who essentially have a mutual problem. Further, when the client consults the lawyer, the client has generally concluded that the marriage is already effectively terminated. The lawyer is too often "the end of the line."

One fundamental difficulty any ecclesiastical organization faces in meeting the over-all problem is the traditional attitude of the Church toward marriage and divorce. Full and frank discussion with any such organization of marital problems that appear to be beyond solution would seem futile to a Catholic who feels that under no circumstance would the Church permit a divorce with a right to remarry.

Both parties may conclude in all sincerity that their marriage is spiritually and definitively terminated. Although they believe that this marriage can be shown to be dead in fact, they know that the Church will not pronounce it dead. For example, today it is not uncommon for one partner to leave the other, move to another jurisdiction, obtain a divorce and marry another with complete legality. Yet the deserted spouse of this dead marriage may not obtain a divorce with the approval of the Church and is permanently barred from marriage and all that it implies so long as the first partner lives.

Many marriages can be saved that may be sick and even dying, but not dead. These might be saved by the utilization of ecclesiastical conciliation courts of the type resembling the secular conciliation court now being used effectively in California and elsewhere, manned and supported by skilled specialists. The California experience will be discussed briefly later.

Secular Court Practice

The divorce problem throughout the nation has been with us for many years. Particularly since World War II the liberalization and addition of statutory grounds for divorce and the broadening interpretation of the older grounds have created a kind of mass production of divorce decrees, some for causes that were not recognized a few generations earlier.

The power of a court to grant a divorce is conferred by statute. The grounds are established by the legislatures of the several states but the interpretation of these grounds is the duty of the courts. The causes for divorce vary from state to state as do the judicial interpretations. Legislators in the various states have added to the older grounds (adultery, impotence and certain kinds of cruelty) other more socially acceptable grounds such as "incompatability" or its equivalent. Divorce indeed has been made easier over the years and that trend will not change in our lifetime.

Until recent years with liberalized legislation the traditional divorce has been an adversary proceeding in which the court finds the defendant (libelee) guilty of marital fault and the plaintiff (libelant) free of fault. However unreal this concept, it has been adhered to faithfully in the "marital fault" states.

The plaintiff in the typical "cruel and abusive conduct" case is normally the wife but on occasion is the husband. The plaintiff's testimony is routinely highly colored and may be perjured, but the court can do little but accept it as the truth since very few cases are contested and since in addition that testimony is usually supported by evidence of the same quality given by a friendly witness. Even in contested cases the intimate nature of the marital relationship makes it extremely difficult to demonstrate that the complaint is without merit. Where cruelty of a physical nature is the required norm, medical evidence or police evidence may be available to the court in a contested case, but where cruelty more and more frequently is interpreted as mental cruelty—in a variety of aspects—the granting of an uncontested divorce is nearly inevitable, and a contest is not likely to result in the defeat of the libel.

The expansion of the concept of "cruelty" is largely the product of judicial decisions in response to the changing attitude of the community, and its general availability (as distinguished from other standard causes such as desertion, adultery or impotence) has made this ground the most readily usable in states that still require marital fault.

Some jurisdictions have done away with marital fault by providing such grounds as "incompatability" or "irreconcilable differences." Others permit divorce where the parties have lived apart for a specified period (one year or two years) pursuant to a written separation agreement. There is much pressure to extend these concepts to the "fault" jurisdictions.

Essentially the courts are concerned that children are cared for properly after divorce and that the wife does not become a burden to the state because of the husband's failure to provide adequately for her, particularly when the children are young. These matters being settled between the parties by written agreement drawn up by lawyers and approved by the court, it is only necessary that adequate evidence be presented in support of the cause alleged in the libel for divorce.

In those relatively rare circumstances when a divorce might prove difficult in the state of the marriage domicile or invite undesirable notoriety, or where the parties simply want a divorce quickly, quietly and unconditionally, one partner moves temporarily to another more suitable jurisdiction and resides there for the time required by its statute. A routine complaint is filed, the other partner who has remained at home enters an appearance through a lawyer, and after pro forma testimony the plaintiff obtains a divorce effective immediately and binding throughout the nation.

All these practices are accepted in the United States. The liberalization of grounds for divorce and the existence of jurisdictions where divorces are made even easier, quicker and quieter are part of the common knowledge of the average citizen. Divorce no longer disturbs. Yet its accelerating growth creates progressively more serious problems for adults and future adults and for the nation.

In recognition of the principle that the state is a party to a divorce, from time to time efforts have been made to force concerned couples to give thought to all the implications of a divorce. Thus, laws have been enacted requiring a period of separation of husband and wife before either may file a libel for divorce. Again, in some states a divorce is not final when granted after hearing, but becomes effective later. Thus, in Massachusetts the decree is granted conditionally and does not become final until six months thereafter. These have been generally meaningless.

The California Experience

However, some laws of relatively recent vintage offer better prospect of success. The State of California is providing a means for couples to obtain sound advice and guidance in marital difficulties. The Los Angeles Conciliation Court was established in 1954 as a department of the Superior Court. Its purpose, as outlined in the Conciliation Court Law, is: ". . . to protect the rights of children and to promote the public welfare by preserving, promoting and protecting family life and the institution of matrimony, and to provide means for the reconciliation of spouses and the amicable settlement of domestic and family controversy."

Thus, this court is not merely a reconciliation court, nor are its conciliation functions compulsory in nature. It attempts by conciliation to resolve marital difficulties as a condition precedent to any formal separation.

Conciliation is under the jurisdiction and control of the court. The judge directs the operations and affairs of the court and presides over hearings under some circumstances. While he is assigned to this court because of his competence and interest in the field of family law, he is not trained as a marriage counselor and does not counsel. This counseling is performed by a staff of highly trained behavioral scientists, each with a Master's Degree as a minimum and at least five years' experience in clinical counseling before joining the court.

In a 1971 report of the effectiveness of the conciliation procedure since 1954, the court announced that 18,255 families were reconciled involving 34,742 children. Three out of four reconciled couples were still living together one year later. Of course, many attempts at conciliation were unsuccessful and divorce proceedings took their normal course.

Following the success of the conciliation courts (whose functions were not disturbed) and reinforcing the idea that courts have a major responsibility to play an active role in strengthening and preserving family life, California enacted its Family Law Act which became effective on January 1, 1970.

This pioneering legislation abolished the adversary system and the principle of fault in a divorce court. The only ground for divorce (apart from incurable insanity) is "irreconcilable differences causing the irremediable breakdown of the marriage."

"Irreconcilable differences" as a ground is not "no fault" divorce or divorce by consent of the parties. The first decision of the California Supreme Court under the new Family Law Act made this clear. In McKim v. McKim the majority opinion interpreted the act as requiring the consideration of the marriage as a whole and making the possibility of reconciliation the important issue to be determined. No decree of dissolution can be granted upon the default of one party or by consent. On the contrary, the court must require proof that the marriage is irretrievable before a decree of dissolution will be granted. Further, the decision states: "Under the Family Law Act the court, not the parties, must decide whether the evidence adduced supports findings that irreconcilable differences do exist and that the marriage has broken down irremediably and should be dissolved."

Admittedly, much depends upon the attitude of the judge.

It would be relatively easy for the judge to find the marriage irretrievable, and it would not be particularly difficult for determined parties to present evidence to justify or even compel a decree of dissolution. Nonetheless, if adequate objective norms can be established, dissolution should not be the product of caprice or a passing grievance. Certainly, reasonable proof that a marriage is dead can be adduced honestly and openly to the satisfaction of a judge utilizing recognized and acceptable principles, and if that proof is required the home and the nation may benefit from this law. Only experience will demonstrate its effectiveness.

Is it possible that the Church might find a study of the California pattern helpful? Certainly the Church's efforts in this area would be on a modest scale, but in today's pluralistic world would some consideration be warranted?

Eugene C. Kennedy, M.M.

Signs of Life
in Marriage

T he following essay concerns itself with a change in the consciousness of the world and the
Church toward marriage. Both have come to perceive it afresh
and to make judgments about it according to a new set of
values. The Church is moving even in its court system from a
legal to an existential model in reflecting on and dealing with
marriage. As it attempts to do this it becomes increasingly
important to understand the human signs which tell us
whether a marriage is alive or not. These signals may be complex and subtle, and they demand a sharpened sensitivity on
the part of the ecclesiastical forum whose business it is to
consider them. These will be reviewed along with the implications of this change in consciousness for the pastoral and
administrative practice of the Church with regard to marriage.

The world has welcomed the greening of the curial Church
which has made itself manifest in its new emphasis on the
reality of the human experience of marriage. This attitude
is one aspect of the Church's over-all rediscovery of the Gospel consciousness of both the limits and possibilities of the
human condition. As Jesus knew what was in man, so now
the administrative Church, more humanly wise and less con-
tent with absolutes, moves back toward man in an understanding and compassionate manner. These moves have been
related to the world's transformation of its own conscious-

121

ness about the nature and values of marriage; indeed, these shifts are themselves intimately inter-related. The Church has modified its view because it has begun to heal its schism with the world and has been able once more to learn from rather than just to sit in judgment on human experience.

Social observers have noted for some time the decline of what has been termed patriarchal marriage, that is, the marriage dominated to a large extent by the man, his supposed needs, and, all too frequently, his shortcomings. This model, which so underplayed the role of the woman and consequently so distorted the male-female paradigm, has crumbled as the absolute need for marriage as an institution has declined. In other words, as marriage has become less important to populate the world and to insure the proper passage of legal rights and titles, persons have come to value it as an expression of the rich possibilities of human sharing rather than as a cure for man's unruly passions. Institution has been subordinated to relationship in the same way that control of man has been subordinated to the affirmation of his free choice and acceptance of marital responsibilities. These shifts reflect a more positive and compassionate view toward man but they also impose a greater burden on the marriage relationship itself. Men and women now look to each other for the rewards of emotional satisfaction and support; the modern consciousness has elevated the marriage relationship to an ideal state in which man and woman may meet, share, and celebrate life in a truly loving fashion.

It is not surprising that the heightened expectations of marriage have caused it to weaken as an institution; this situation is aggravated at the present time because of the social and emotional isolation in which many families live. They depend very much on the small circle they constitute together, and while at times the rewards may be great, the disappointments can also be intense and damaging. Marriage is under strain, not because people want to abandon it but because they want to make a success of it, not because they think it is inhuman but because they look on it as one of their only opportunities to become fully human themselves. The common notion that marriage is declining in popularity or in vigor as an ideal of stabilized inter-personal relationship is simply not sustained by any close inspection of what is occurring in contemporary America. Rather we see people more interested in marriage than ever and far more interested in the quality of marriage than in the fact of marriage; they are, therefore, more ready to make judgments about the life or death of a marriage instead of carrying it on because of the binding force of the legal institution which once persuaded them they had no other choice.

People keep getting married, and even those who get divorced keep getting married because they want the rewards that seem to them to come from a successful marriage. These rewards are largely psychological in nature, but they have come to be identified as those of greatest value to human beings. Men have also come to recognize the religious dimension in this close human experience, one that has been long recognized by the Church and which has been underscored in our own day in a wide variety of theological affirmations of the significance of marriage. Within this shift we find man and woman beginning to stand on a more equal footing with each other and trying to understand and explore their common humanity with a subtlety and sophistication that has hardly been known before in the history of mankind.

In the United States the canon lawyers have been prominent in their willingness to investigate and make concrete a new and more humane appreciation for the qualities of the marriage relationship. This is a traditional theological stance, of course, because it focuses on what the man and woman mean to each other, on what they truly exchange at the moment when they administer the sacrament of marriage to each other. The Church has always recognized, in other words, that it is something about the quality of the intention and motivation of the man and woman which determines the presence or absence of a true marriage. There is nothing startlingly new in the Church's present return to this concept. It is in harmony with its best understanding of what marriage can and should be. To approach marriage with this sensitivity does, however, cause practical problems and requires a contemporary refinement of the Church's ability to judge the presence or absence of realized human values in the marriage relationship.

If the Church, through its administrators, is to respond to man in his search for richer and better marriage relationships, then it must acquaint itself with the psychological realities and the needs of the behavior which for so long it has taken as the basis for its judgment about marriage. This represents a transformation of the theoretical model which the Church employs in its pastoral and administrative practice concerning marriage. Part of the struggle for the lawyers of the Church at the present time is to move effectively from a legal to an existential model. This raises urgent practical questions because of the complications implicit in this shift of models. It requires the Church to change its basic manner of viewing and making judgments about marriage. The new model demands attention to psychological realities that have always been notoriously difficult for judicial systems, no matter how sophisticated, to integrate successfully into the application of law. This issue will be discussed later; for the moment, it is essential to review some of the existential aspects of human relationships which we have learned, through research, to be vital signs, that is, the signals that marriage relationships are living and effective. The living relationships, the vital exchange: this is the idea on which all meaningful marriage is built; it also illustrates the parameters of judgment which must be employed by those who wish to make wise and appropriate human decisions in questions concerning the marriage relationship.

Most of the research that we have on the quality of relationships arises from examining psychotherapeutic relationships. It is presumed that good therapy relationships, which can be studied carefully and judged as to their effectiveness, are essentially reflections of what must be found in any good human relationships. The experience of therapy is thought to give a heightened experience of the values that reside in any good human relationship. It does not offer anything essentially different from what is found, whether in friendship or marriage, when people make some genuine loving difference to each other. What we do understand from research on marriage tells us that marriages can be classified on a continuum of vital relatedness. In other words, both common sense and research tell us that marriages may be rated according to the reality and the depth of the personal exchange that takes place between the man and woman. The nature of the intimacy they share—or whether there is any sharing at all—shows through the style of their relating with each other. There are many easily readable signs that tell whether this man and woman have ever reached each other in an authentic way, whether their communication has gone beyond the reciprocal registration of complaints, or whether they have ever really been lovingly present to each other as persons. The test of the marriage relationship is the test of any good relationship: whether those who are partners to it are able to enlarge each other's lives or not. This quality of relationship is very difficult to judge on legal grounds alone; it may be impossible to write it into a judicial opinion, but unless there is some appreciation of these vital signs, no decision, even if it is sealed seven-fold, can speak to the human experiential base of marriage.

To telescope briefly the chief signs of a living relationship is to reveal the opposite side of the coin of what the canonists call "moral impotence." If these qualities seem present in a reasonable degree, then there is a strong argument in favor of a valid marriage. If, however, for whatever reason, it is clear that these are not present, or that there has been too much immaturity shown by one or both partners ever to make these a reality, then it is an equally reasonable decision to say that no marriage exists.

The first of these qualities is genuineness or authenticity. It implies that the real person of the man and the real person of the woman are actually present in the relationship of marriage. This does not mean that they must be psychologically present to a perfect degree, nor does it rule out growth over the years. It does, however, mean that the individual man and woman must be in sufficient possession of their own identity at the time of their marriage so that they can be described as knowing who they are and possessing the capability of revealing themselves to each other. To reduce this to concrete language, the individual must not be so lost in his own needs, so absorbed in his own psychological structure, that he never truly perceives the other as separate from him and from his own emotional distortions. It is altogether too common, especially for very young people whose identities are by no means formed, to approach marriage, not with a clear view of each other, but with an image of each other that has been projected from their own inner needs. When this is the case—and this is almost always true for individuals who have not yet successfully completed the psychological tasks of their adolescent growth—then it may be judged existentially that this man and woman have not been truly present to each other.

Obviously there are many gradations of the kind of presence which people with still developing personalities are capable of in their relationships with each other. For a marriage to be contracted sacramentally, there is surely a minimal kind of presence which must be demanded. The man and woman must be in contact with each other not just sexually and not even just socially; they must know more than the facts about each other's lives. This quality of psychological presence demands some evidence that they have achieved an adequate sense of themselves and of their own sexual identity, that their motivations are reasonably clear and that their goals in life have a fairly definite form. These would be some of the indications favoring the judgment of sufficient psychological presence for a true marriage. Many other factors can impede this, including a wide range of inner needs, many of which are intensified by the pressure of current romantic ideals.

Many young people are criticized for entering into unions which are marriage-like even though they are not blessed by the law or the Church. In fact, however, sometimes these young people do recognize that they are not yet in sufficient possession of themselves to be present to each other in a way that would be enduring. The fact that they want to make their arrangement tentative is probably good evidence of their awareness that they have yet to develop the fullness of mutual presence required in marriage. There may be more wisdom than mischief in such judgments.

Genuineness, however, describes a quality which is humanly recognizable even when it is not legally provable. We know instinctively whether or not another person has made his true self present to us in life just as we recognize when we are investing or holding our own selves back from a particular relationship. A sensitive observer can tell the difference between the relationships of persons who are in contact with each other and those who are merely rubbing their defenses against each other. It takes time and effort to reconstruct the psychological climate of a relationship, but it is not impossible to do this. In making this kind of judgment, however, one must not expect a full and perfect kind of psychological presence at the time of marriage. What should be expected is an adequate meeting of the people involved but one which leaves a good deal of room for their further development and for their further self-disclosure to each other. What is needed, in other words, is the evidence of a good psychological beginning—that these two persons see each other in reasonably good focus even though they may tend somewhat to idealize each other, that nothing inhibits them in a major way from revealing, insofar as their self-awareness allows, the truth about themselves to each other.

A second characteristic of good relationships is described as empathy, a word that has become almost too faddish to employ successfully in this regard. It refers to a person's capacity to make himself or herself present to the other. Empathy suggests not only that a person is capable of revealing himself but that he can also perceive the other as separate from him. It suggests that he can understand the other's view of the world even though it is different to some extent from his own. Empathy is first-hand evidence that a person has been able to pierce his own psychological armor, that he has been able to see the world without the distortions that he might ordinarily impose upon it because of his own emotional needs, that he can, in other words, see into the life of another person and appreciate it as non-alien territory. Empathy is a test of whether individuals can put aside their own concerns enough to understand each other in a profoundly personal way. If a person lacks the capacity to grasp the world of another, he is surely incapable of contracting a valid marriage. When, however, it is clear that two individuals have a feeling for each other that enables them to see and appreciate their differences as well as their similarities, we observe one of the vital signs of true marriage. This is the cornerstone of the concept of communication about which so much is made in all the commentaries on marriage. Unless individuals have this talent of understanding, all their communications are made in one direction; without the skill and human interest in listening to each other, they are in one-sided relationships where nothing of a reciprocal nature takes place. Everything that we treasure in the traditions of the Church and mankind about marriage rests on this ability to reach out and touch the world of another person with our own understanding. When a person has never grown far enough away from his own needs and interests, he imposes his own meanings on what the other says or does; this is all too often what characterizes marriages in which the man and woman have not been truly present to each other. The test of their presence comes in the challenge of empathy. A man and woman need not be able to do this perfectly either, but they must demonstrate the capacity for it. Sometimes their one-sided testimony to a marriage counselor is sufficient proof of their inability to empathize.

Healthy relationships that are marked by the exchange of

life are also characterized by what has come to be termed non-possessive caring or regard. One would naturally expect this quality to obtain in a marriage relationship where, presumably, the man and woman love each other or would never propose to marry in the first place. People do funny things, however, and it is relatively easy to mistake immature emotional involvement and the projection of romantic needs for the deep and simple kind of love that is marriage's most vital sign. The richness of the couple's sexual life springs from the genuineness of this quality. The success of a couple in adjusting to each other as well as to the stresses and pains of life depends on whether this quality exists or not. Too many people admit later on that they were once in love with someone; they mourn their loves, falling in and out of them with ease. The kind of love that is a vital sign of marriage is not quite so fragile or mercurial. It demands a certain amount of maturity and follows upon an individual's capacity for psychological presence and successful empathy.

These qualifications come in clusters; you do not find genuine love if the other elements are lacking. In the same way, if the other elements are present, then it is almost always authentic love that binds a couple together in an effective manner. Indeed, one cannot understand the mystery of non-possessive love unless one includes the concept of the other two vital signs. These may, in the long run, be the best test of whether the love is actually genuine or not. These other conditions imply the kind of vulnerability and willingness to share which are essentially bound up with what we understand about enduring love. Enduring love implies that individuals perceive each other as separate and yet as bound together or committed to each other in a unique way. It means that they have overcome their own self-centeredness to the point where they can give themselves to the good of each other above their own good. It also suggests that they are trying to free each other for fuller life rather than to possess each other just for themselves. This kind of love, in other words, is probably not present if the relationship is marked by excessive fear, jealousy, or an unwillingness to allow the other to be separate and distinct as an individual human being.

These characteristics, along with their concrete expression in various ways in the lives of people who contract marriage, are the best existential signs that we now know of about whether the marriage is alive or not. These factors are sensitively inter-related so that a failure in one is bound to affect the individual's responses in the others. The presence of these characteristics tells us that the man and woman enjoy a healthy intimacy with each other and that they are sufficiently adult and knowing to contract a valid marriage. The major failure of any of these factors could well constitute presumptive evidence that the marriage was never a meeting of two separate people but a fusion of needs which would have to go by some other name than that of sacramental marriage. The grasp of these qualities enables us to assist marriages which are in distress because we can help people to recapture these qualities if it is clear that they once possessed them. It is, however, far more difficult to generate these in relationships where they have never been present. While these signs could be elaborated on in much greater detail, these descriptions are sufficient for the present discussion. They are signs of life, but it is very difficult to write laws about these or for a judicial forum to make adequate judgments concerning their presence or absence.

Many questions flow from a consideration of these vital signs of marriage. They are connected with the Church's program of education, its willingness to validate the man-woman relationship as a model for the richest and best of human relationships, as well as for the implementation of effective marriage counseling programs which are built on the religious values implicit in these vital signs of human relationships. These signs offer the Church a solid base for developing a kind of creative faithfulness that allows man and woman to continue to make themselves present, to reach out with understanding, and to affirm each other with their love.

This shift to the quality of the marriage relationship does, however, challenge the legal model which the Church has, for so many centuries, used almost exclusively in its dealings with Christian marriage. This legal code, like all legal codes, has its clutch of exceptions in various privileges and traditions which have become incorporated into the administration of the law. There are those in the Church now who say that these exceptions and the already extant canonical methodology of the Church offer ample room for dealing with marriage legally in a freshly human way, and that, even by the law alone, many more marriages could be annulled than we have previously been willing to admit. Some research has, in fact, shown that one of the determinants of the effective canonical remedy for marriages in distress is the interest and the aggressiveness of the parish priest in pursuing the case. There may be, in other words, many genuine opportunities to apply existential understanding to the marriage laws of the Church. It may be, however, that the contemporary transformation of ecclesiastical consciousness has moved it irretrievably beyond the legal framework. Simply put, the developing attitude perceives marriage as a fundamentally existential rather than a legal situation; it moves beneath the external behavior which has traditionally been employed as a basis for the Church's inferences and attempts to comprehend and incorporate practically the far more ambiguous realities of psychological motivation, presence, and exchange. It may not be clear to some ecclesiastical lawgivers that they are moving so rapidly into this rather different model of human relationships; it is nevertheless an inevitable move for those who see the category of moral impotence as a broad and appropriate designation of the psychological facts of many apparently dead marriages. The widening application of this concept of moral impotence, the increased use of the judgments of psychological and psychiatric experts, the unwillingness on the part of many canon lawyers to make a legal loophole game out of what comes down to a question of existential truth or falsehood: these are signals that the formerly rather secure legal process is itself under considerable distress.

Canon lawyers are attempting to face this issue squarely in order to move to the logical conclusion of their new awareness of the many-layered complications of the human relationship that is Christian marriage. It may be that it is time to consider far more seriously the suggestion that already has been made many times to separate the judgment about the validity of marriage from the ecclesiastical tribunals and to give it to some forum that is broadly representative of the Christian community itself. In other words, the canonical courts could deal with the legal effects of judgments about validity which are made in a far more flexible and human manner by the delegates of the Christian community. These groupings could, of course, include appropriate medical and social science experts, but their core strength would reside in the persons whose own maturity enables them to make judgments about the presence or absence of the vital signs of the marriage relationship. This would be, in effect, a common-sense judgment about the particular marriage relationship under consideration. Such common-sense judgments may, in fact, be exactly what the Church needs if it is to incorporate this new sensitivity into its practical pastoral service to mankind. Common-sense judgments are not, after all, to be under-rated; they really echo the judgment of the community which is common sense in its fundamental meaning.

To relocate the judgment about the reality of marriage in the community of believers is essential on two counts. First of all, it recognizes the proper personal viewpoint that is essential for understanding marriage. In the long run only the man and woman can tell us if their marriage is alive or dead; only they can give voice to what they have known in their life together. The dynamics of current theological reflection on marriage are moving in the direction of validating this perception of marriage. The theologizing Church is retreating from the legal heights that enabled it self-confidently to look down on and make absolute judgments about experiential realities of which it had little knowledge. Even the right to make these judgments will soon be questioned within the Church. In any case, the Christian community offers the best human setting for married people to seek the truth of their own relationship. Within a very few years any other attitude will be considered somewhat sacrilegious. The time, then, is ripe to prepare the Church for a more personal and ultimately more religious handling of marriage cases.

Secondly, the presence of the Christian community makes the Church itself present to married couples in the richest and most loving way possible. Putting aside the robes of the judge, the Church is able to become a more genuine witness to the realities of Christian marriage. The responsibility of the couple will be heightened, but they will have the human and spiritual resources of the Church available to them through this special reflective grouping of fellow Christians. The Church, in other words, will be a continuing source of strength and support for the man and woman who are sounding the depths of their own relationship. Only through an effective personal approach can the Church fulfill its own responsibilities to the sacramental significance of marriage. To put it simply, only this course will enable the Church to maintain effective and helpful contact with contemporary man as he searches out an understanding of the experience of marriage. The coming generation may well take away any choices the administrative Church could now freely make about its manner of dealing with marriage. The Church has been left to catch up too often; now is the time to understand the vital experiential signs of marriage and to create the community forums in which a living theology of marriage can effectively be applied.

Lawrence G. Wrenn

Marriage— Indissoluble or Fragile?

L ately I have been reading Sacred Scripture and the Fathers of the Church and popes and councils and Penitentials on the subject of divorce and remarriage, and it seems to me that there are in these sources two quite distinct traditions: the first that divorce and remarriage are not *permitted* and the second that they are not *possible*. The first tradition would say that a remarriage after divorce is not *licit;* the second would say that it is not *valid*.

It is, of course, the second school which is now firmly in possession, the school which teaches that marriage involves an objective, indissoluble, perpetual, life-long bond, a bond (*vinculum*) which is broken only by death, so that if the parties separate and either attempts to remarry, that attempt is a non-marriage. It is null and void because of the diriment impediment of prior bond (*ligamen*).

Once the issue becomes firmly embedded within that framework, then the framework tends to get between us and reality. It conditions our perceptions and distorts or colors our sensations. Reality does not come through clean. So, for example, when we read the Gospel texts on divorce and remarriage, we hear Jesus saying that marriage is absolutely indissoluble, whereas, in fact, it is entirely possible that he is not really saying that at all.

134

First of all Jesus does not use the word "indissoluble," and secondly, if the phrase "marriage is indissoluble" means that marriage establishes and/or is established by some unbreakable bond, then a clean reading of the words of Christ does not necessarily involve him in that issue at all. It may be that Jesus is just roundly denouncing divorce and severely prohibiting it, but not necessarily declaring it impossible.

Jesus, for example, could have said: "What God has joined together man *cannot* put asunder." But he did not say that. Instead he said: "*Let not* man put asunder," as though he was acknowledging the ability of man to break the bond but at the same time enjoining him not to do so.

The other assertion of Jesus, "Whoever divorces his wife and marries another commits adultery against her," could certainly be interpreted to include implicitly the notion of an indissoluble bond (he commits adultery against her precisely because he is still married to her in spite of the divorce), but on the other hand, the clear thrust of Christ's remark is not to declare the second marriage invalid but to accuse the man of being unfaithful and unjust to his first wife, to prohibit divorce and remarriage as being against the commandments of God. It is, in other words, a moral teaching rather than a determination of juridical status.

No doubt many of us *hear* the words of Jesus as a determination of juridical status, but I suspect that this is largely a result of our unconsciously superimposing a juridical mentality onto a neutral setting.

The distortion, I think, is not in seeing a bond where there is none but in seeing the bond as indissoluble whereas in fact it is quite fragile. Few people would doubt that marriage involves a union or bond between a man and a woman, a joining of those two people. The question is whether that union or bond or joining is unbreakable. It does not seem to me that Jesus is declaring it to be such. Rather he appears to be attaching a seal to marriage that says in effect: Warning! Fragile! Handle with care! Do not bend, fold or mutilate!

Jesus, in other words, was not declaring divorce and remarriage to be invalid but only illicit.

On the other hand, this is a long way from saying, as some have said, that Christ's matrimonial teaching is merely an ideal. An ideal, I take it, is a standard of *perfection,* a *model* for us to live by. But surely Christ is saying more than that. He is enunciating, it seems to me, not an ideal but a principle, that is to say, a standard of *goodness,* a *rule* of behavior.

In the context of George MacRae's chapter, this is, no doubt, the way in which Matthew and Paul interpreted their master's teaching on marriage. If, on the one hand, they had understood Christ to be declaring that marriage creates an indissoluble bond between the spouses which invalidates any attempt at a second marriage, then they would hardly have felt free to introduce modifications, since a modification would have involved their permitting the impossible, that is to say, their declaring licit what was not valid. And if, on the other hand, they had viewed Christ's words only as a call to an ideal, then it is not likely that they would have been so chary of their indulgence.

Clearly Matthew and Paul understood Jesus to be declaring a principle or rule of conduct. All they did then was to recognize exceptions to that principle.

This interpretation likewise explains some of the statements and attitudes of churchmen through the ages. Tertullian, for example, before he became a Montanist, said, in about the year 207:

But observe, if this Christ be yours when he teaches contrary to Moses and the creator, on the same principle must he be mine, if I can show that his teaching is not contrary to them. I maintain, then, that there was a condition in the prohibition which he now made of divorce, the case supposed being that a man put away his wife for the express purpose of marrying another. His words are: "Whoever puts away his wife, and marries another, commits adultery: and whoever marries her that is put away from her husband also commits adultery." "Put away," that is, for the reason wherefore a woman ought not to be dismissed, that another wife may be obtained. For he who marries a woman who is unlawfully put away is as much of an adulterer as the man who marries one who is undivorced. Permanent is the marriage which is not rightly dissolved; to marry, therefore, while matrimony is undissolved, is to commit adultery. Since, therefore, his prohibition of divorce was a conditional one, he did not prohibit absolutely; and what he did not absolutely forbid, that he permitted on some occasions, where there is an absence of the cause why he gave this prohibition. In very deed his teaching is not contrary to Moses, whose precept he partially defends, I will not say confirms.[1]

Some thirty-five or forty years later, Origen of Alexandria said:

But now contrary to what was written, even some of the rulers of the Church have permitted a woman to marry, even when her husband was living, doing contrary to what was written, where it said, "A wife is bound for so long as her husband lives," and "Therefore a woman is called an adulteress if she be with another man while her husband lives." Yet they did not take the step altogether without reason. It would seem that they make this concession, contrary though it is to the law established at the creation and contained in Scripture, as the lesser of two evils.[2]

Then, in the first decade of the fourth century, just about a hundred years after Tertullian, we hear Lactantius, the tutor of Constantine's son, bemoaning but nevertheless admitting the fragility of the marriage bond in the words: "Whoever breaks apart the joining of the body is regarded as an adulterer." The fuller text reads as follows:

For such is not the case, as is the interpretation of public law, that she alone is the adulteress who has another man, while the male is free from the charge of adultery, though he have many mistresses. The divine law so joins the two with equal right into a marriage, which is two in one flesh, that whoever breaks apart the joining of the body is regarded as an adulterer. . . . But, however, lest anyone think that he is able to circumscribe the divine precepts, there are added these points, that all calumny and chance for fraud be removed; he is an adulterer who takes a wife who has been sent away by her husband; and so is he who has, aside from the crime of adultery, put a wife away that he may take another. God did not intend for the "one flesh" to be separated and torn apart.[3]

In the year 375, St. Basil the Great, bishop of Caesarea, noted, as regards the innocent husband:

In the case of a husband who has been abandoned it will be necessary to examine the cause for the desertion. If it is manifest that the woman left without justification, the husband [the clear implication here is that the husband has remarried] is worthy of forgiveness and the woman deserves punishment. Forgiveness will be accorded to such a husband provided he is in communion with the Church.[4]

And even when it comes to the guilty husband, that is, the husband who has abandoned his wife and married another, Basil notes a tradition which permits the man to be reconciled to the Church after penance. He says:

He who has deserted a woman with whom he was lawfully united in order to take another is certainly subject to condemnation as an adulterer in virtue of the sentence of the Lord; but it was decided by our Fathers that the culpable ones shall do penance as mourners for one year, as hearers for two years, as kneelers for three years, and that on the seventh year they shall stand with the faithful and they shall be judged worthy of the offering if they have done penance with tears.[5]

In the year 726 Pope Gregory II, in a letter to St. Boniface, wrote:

You have asked what is a husband to do if his wife, having been afflicted with an infirmity, cannot have sexual intercourse with the husband. It would be good if he could remain as he is and practice abstinence. But since this requires great virtue, if he cannot live chastely, it is better if he marry. Let him, however, not stop supporting her, since she is kept from married life by her infirmity and not by a detestable fault.[6]

Perhaps it was Gregory whom Pope Alexander III had particularly in mind when he wrote during his papacy (1159-1181):

If legitimate marital consent takes place between a man and a woman in such a way that each receives the other by mutual consent expressed in the usual words, whether confirmed by an oath or not, then it is not licit for the man to marry another woman. And if he does marry, even if they have sexual relations, they should be compelled by ecclesiastical penalty to be separated from each other and return to their former spouses. I say this even though I know that others feel differently about it and that indeed the matter was judged differently by our own predecessors.[7]

But even though Alexander is disagreeing with Gregory, it is interesting that first of all he speaks of the more liberal opinion as having been held by certain of his predecessors (*"a quibusdam praedecessoribus nostris"*), in the plural; and secondly that Alexander himself, who was described by John Noonan as a "professor of Canon Law at the University of Bologna, veteran curialist, chancellor of the Roman Church, and the first master of Canon Law to rule as pope,"[8] indicated only that it would not be *licit* for the man to remarry (*"non licet mulieri alii nubere"*). The master of canon law did not suggest that the marriage would be invalid.

Of course, all of these citations, from Tertullian in the year 207 through Alexander III almost a thousand years later, represent only one tradition, the illiceity tradition. Meanwhile, though, the invalidity tradition, certainly more imposing but not necessarily more correct, grew up alongside it, and within a short time after Alexander's death it practically dominated the Church. It was just around this time that marriage was, for the first time, officially recognized as a "sacrament" (a term that had always carried overtones of perpetuity) on the same footing as baptism, the Eucharist and the sacrament of penance.[9] These were also the days of the Schoolmen, of Gratian and Ivo of Chartres and Peter Lombard and Hugh of St. Victor who all agreed that marriage was indissoluble and who went therefore to the further question as to what constituted marriage: consent or consummation.

By 1439 Pope Eugene IV, in his *Decree for the Armenians*, required the Armenians to agree to the indissolubility of the bond of marriage.[10] And in 1563, at the twenty-fourth session of the Council of Trent, it was decreed:

If anyone says that the Church errs when it taught and does teach, according to evangelical and apostolic doctrine, that the bond of marriage is not able to be dissolved on account of the adultery of either party and that neither of them, not even the innocent one who was not the cause of the adultery, is able to contract another marriage while the other spouse is still living; and that he who has taken another after dismissing the adulteress, and she who has married another after dismissing the adulterer, commits adultery, let him be anathema.[11]

A footnote in Denziger calls attention to the fact that the rather convoluted phrasing of this canon, resulting in the anathematizing only of those who accuse the Church of erring, was in deference to the Greeks who did not so accuse the Church but nevertheless held another opinion themselves, and this question has been treated at some length elsewhere.[12] But the point is that, for whatever reason, Trent made no solemn statement declaring the bond of marriage to be indissoluble.

Nevertheless the indissolubility-invalidity tradition (the first marriage is indissoluble, the second invalid) won the day and became more and more accepted as the official Catholic teaching on marriage. Be that as it may, this chapter and perhaps even this book is a plea to restudy and to revive the fragility-illiceity tradition (the first marriage is a fragile union which needs special care; to break it and enter a second marriage is against the will of God and is gravely illicit).

Several reasons would seem to warrant giving our most serious and urgent attention to this study. For one thing the fragility-illiceity tradition is an ancient and honorable one endorsed by popes and saints and bishops and the Fathers of the Church and obviously in widespread use in the Church over extended periods of time. The Penitentials or Penitential Books are probably the best witness to this. These Penitentials were little manuals or handbooks for the confessor designed to assist him in determining the gravity of a sin and in assigning a suitable penance. Historically it appears that, for the first five or six centuries, penance in the Church was largely public. This involved being a mourner or hearer or kneeler, as mentioned earlier by St. Basil. But in the fifth or sixth century the practice of assigning private penance began in Ireland, Wales and Britain, and later spread to the continent. In those days the sacraments were generally administered by the abbot of a monastery and the priest-monks. And probably for the sake of some reasonable degree of uniformity in practice, the abbot or some learned monk wrote a Penitential for the use of all the confessors.

These were, of course, turbulent days. The barbarians had over-run Europe and were now being converted to Christianity, and they brought their own customs with them. The old days of the empire appeared staid and orderly in comparison. The poor Irish monks were faced with a bewildering gamut of problems.

But the Church adapted. When it came to the question of divorce and remarriage, many of the Penitentials, particularly during the seventh and eighth centuries, simply followed the tradition of Matthew and Paul, the illiceity tradition, and added new exceptions of their own, tailored to the times.

The *Penitential of Cummean,* for example, dating from the middle of the seventh century (Cummean was probably the Abbot of Iona), contains the following:

However, one spouse can grant permission to the other to enter the service of God in a monastery and he himself can remarry. If he or she was in a first marriage, this is not canonical according to the Greek usage only; but if in a second marriage, he or she is not permitted to contract a third marriage during the lifetime of the spouse.[13]

And in the *Penitential of Theodore,* Archbishop of Canterbury, dating from about the same time, we read:

If a slaveman or a slavewoman has been joined in matrimony by the master of both, and later the slaveman or the slavewoman has become free, if he or she who remains in slavery cannot be bought free, the free spouse is permitted to marry a free person.[14]

And again, from the same source:

To him whose wife has been taken away by the enemy, if he cannot retrieve her, it is permitted to take another wife; it is better to do this than to commit fornication. And if she returns later, he is not obliged to receive her back if he has another. She herself may take another husband if she had only one before.[15]

All this business about entering a monastery or being freed from slavery or taken into captivity was a challenge to the Church. But the Church adapted. It was not a matter of compromise. Adaptability is not necessarily weakness. It was simply that the Church had an adaptable framework to function with and it was not afraid to use it.

But all of this about the Penitentials has, to some extent, been a digression. I was saying that one of the reasons why we ought to consider reviving the fragility-illiceity tradition is simply that for centuries it was considered by many Christians to be both acceptable and useful. It is true, of course, that during the second millennium, particularly the second half of that millennium, her sibling and rival tradition has won our exclusive favor, and no doubt for many good reasons. But surely one of those reasons has been merely experiential. I mean that divorce was extremely rare, and we *experienced* marriage as a very stable, virtually indissoluble union.

Not only that, but it was a stable union in a relatively stable society. Not that there weren't wars and revolutions. Not that everybody sat around and rocked. But still there was a continuity with the past and a respect for tradition and a pace of life that was conducive to stability. So it was an atmosphere congenial to the indissolubility tradition.

But our experience is quite different. You don't have to have read Alvin Toffler to know that ours is a throw-away society and the age of transience. This is frighteningly, at least sometimes frighteningly, apparent to the most casual observer. Nor has the institution of marriage been able to isolate itself from its slippery surroundings. It is well known that in the United States one out of every three marriages now ends in divorce and, according to John Charles Wynn, when Catholics marry, their chances are only slightly better.

And the ever increasing de facto fragility of marriage is only half the problem. The other half, the more fundamental and basic half, is that the very nature of marriage seems to be undergoing some kind of metamorphosis. Andrew Greeley, Helen McDaniel and Bernard Häring all discuss the shifting substance of marriage: from the basic unit of production and education entered into by a legal contract concerned mostly with the transmission of the family farm or whatever, to what it is at present, namely the chief source of emotional satisfaction involving a profound inter-personal commitment. Meanwhile, the extended family has given way to the nuclear family, and now the nuclear family seems to be giving at least some ground to the commune and other family types.

In short, marriage is a changing part of a changing world. Thus it is very difficult if not impossible for the people of our time to view marriage as something endowed with a kind of ultimate stability. That kind of stability is simply alien to our experience. It could be argued, of course, that now is precisely the time to emphasize stability and indissolubility, that deep down these are the things our world craves. But that is a tactical approach, and if it comes to that, then most people, I think, will agree that the "Try it, you'll like it" approach can only impress people either as an attempt to impose personal preferences or as a blind adherence to a sterile and anachronistic idol. In either case the Church is bound to lose her audience because they won't even understand what she is talking about. And how then shall we preach the Gospel?

We would do much better, it seems to me, if we would only recognize that ours is an age of turmoil, having much in common with the post-empire days, and that it behooves us therefore to adapt as did the Irish missioners of the seventh and eighth centuries.

Besides, perhaps it is time to face the fact that, at least in the United States, the tribunals are just not equipped to handle or even to summarily review a reasonable percentage of the vast number of cases that deserve attention. Over the past several years the Canon Law Society of America has done yeoman service in obtaining from Rome the approval of a set of procedural norms that have literally revolutionized the tribunals of the United States and permitted them to operate with considerable efficiency. But with all of that and with all of the hard work and dedication of hundreds of tribunal personnel around the country, the results have only pointed up the impotence of the system. During 1971 the United States tribunals annulled or prepared for dissolution something less than 3,000 apparently valid marriages. Perhaps twice that many people received a preliminary but probably reasonable hearing as to the merits of their case, so that it might be said that about nine or ten thousand people had their cases reviewed by a tribunal during the year. This, I suppose, sounds fairly impressive, but it must be remembered that during that same period something like 120,000 civil divorces were granted from presumably valid marriages of Catholics.

I arrive at that figure of "something like 120,000" in the following way. During 1971 the annual divorce rate in the United States was 3.5 per thousand population. (By May 1972 it had risen to 4.1).[16] If Catholics maintained that rate, with a United States Catholic population of 48,390,990 there would have been 169,368 divorces. That figure, however, would be high, mostly for two reasons. First, it is probably true that the Catholic divorce rate lags slightly behind the rest of the country, and if we were to reckon the Catholic divorce rate at 3 rather than 3.5, then the figure would not be 169,368 but 145,170. Secondly, a percentage of those marriages were contracted outside the Church to begin with and may therefore be declared null by simple administrative decree. But what percentage? Well, the 1971 marriage rate in the United States was 10.6 per thousand population. At that rate Catholics entered 512,944 marriages. The Kenedy Directory, however, indicates that in 1971 there were, in fact, only 426,309 Catholic marriages, which means that, statistically anyway, Catholics entered 86,635 marriages outside the Church. This would mean that 17% of marriages entered by Catholics are outside the Church. So of the 145,170 marriages that ended in divorce in 1971, only 83% or 120,491 were presumably valid marriages.

We are dealing, of course, with extrapolation and approximation, but the conclusion "something like 120,000" is, I think, fairly accurate.

Of course there would not be a petitioner for each of those 120,000 divorces. But if Catholics generally were aware of the existence of tribunals, then surely, or at least hopefully, most of those people who had married in the Church and whose marriages had failed would want to obtain a solution from their Church if possible. Even if there were only 100,000 petitioners, we would have given a reasonable hearing to only 10% of the prospective cases.

Nor is that the whole problem. Obviously those people who did not get a hearing last year do not just disappear. They accumulate. And year after year we get further and further behind, so that in a very few years it is no longer 10% of the people who are getting a hearing but 1%. This is quicksand. The more you struggle, the deeper you sink.

But let me sum up. I think what I have been trying to say over these past few pages is that the fragility-illiceity tradition urgently deserves adoption, at least in the United States, for three basic reasons: (1) it is a legitimate tradition, (2) it is timely and functional, and (3) the alternative is, for this time and place, both meaningless and dysfunctional.

If the Church did, in fact, accomplish this kind of renaissance (which would, for me, be one more proof in a long line of proofs that the Church is indeed endowed with a certain eternal youth as the result of the indwelling of the Spirit), then, of course, many significant changes would result in our attitudes and practices, of which I should like to discuss two.

For one thing the critical judgment would be made, for the most part, not by a tribunal but by the parish priest, aided perhaps by a board of lay people. Occasionally, of course, someone might request that his or her marriage actually be declared null, and such petitions could still be handled by tribunals pretty much as they are now. But for the most part the issue would not be whether the marriage was valid or invalid but rather whether the marriage continues to exist or has de facto died or been broken. The first judgment to be made, in other words, would concern itself with whether or not "the marriage has irremediably broken down," whether the parties are "estranged beyond reconciliation." Following that, the priest would have to concern himself with whether his parishioner was repentant for the part he or she played in the failure of the marriage, whether there was religious regret that the marriage had either never become or had ceased to be a genuine sign of Christ's love for his Church, whether all obligations pending from the former marriage were being responsibly met, and whether the difficulties of the past had been resolved and the person was now prepared to enter a new marriage as a covenant relationship.

It must be remembered that the principal forces of marital dissolution in our time are no longer captivity or slavery or monastic vocation but rather something akin to what Eugene Kennedy refers to as the absence of genuineness, empathy or non-possessive caring. These are the things that kill or abort marriage in our time. Perhaps we shall need a new set of Penitential Books written by wise and experienced pastors who know their people and the problems of their people. Timely determinations will have to be made as to what exceptions are to be admitted to the rule of Christ that "whoever divorces his wife and marries another commits adultery against her; and if she divorces her husband and marries another, she commits adultery." But surely the Spirit will assist us to make these determinations.

When the parish priest or parish board judges that the person is disposed to enter a second marriage "in the Lord," then, of course, the marriage would be permitted in the Church. But where it was judged otherwise and the person went through a ceremony anyway, outside the Church, then a separate judgment would have to be made regarding the worthiness of that person to receive the Eucharist.

All of these judgments would be pastoral ones, perhaps what Eugene Kennedy would call "common-sense judgments." But at the same time, as Vernon Bourke pointed out, they might well constitute genuine jurisprudence and have as their inspiration equity, which is the highest form of justice.

This then would be the first result of reintroducing the fragility-illiceity tradition: shifting the judgment from the tribunal to the parish, where alone the volume of cases could be handled. An obvious by-product of that would be to free marriage from the artificial and legalistic straitjacket in which we have confined it and to permit it to become a sacrament again and to stand or fall on its own merit, on whether it is or is not a true sign of Christ's love for his people. It would, in other words, allow mystery to enter marriage again, and perhaps then we would understand a little better what St. Paul meant when he called marriage a "great mystery," a *"magnum sacramentum."*

The second result of accepting the fact that marriages die would seem at least as important as the first. This would involve a shift of emphasis—off the dead marriage and on to the alive one or the struggling one or the soon to be born one. We must come soon to the realization that it is the bond, not the bondage, that is important, that if we are genuinely interested in making marriage less dissoluble, then the most effective way to do that is not to insist on the bondage of marriage but to strengthen its bonds.

Young people, for example, must be made as aware as possible of what they're really doing when they marry, not only so that they can marry in a holy way but so that they can marry in a human way. They have to be helped to see themselves, to see why they're marrying, what rewards they're seeking or what needs they're reaching out to satisfy. And somebody must make it painfully clear to them that the funny little rhyme "Glances that over cocktails seemed so sweet are much less thrilling over shredded wheat" is not just a funny little rhyme.

But is is not just young people who need help. And it is not just preparing people before marriage that is important. It is a total family program that is needed, and the Church—that is, we Christians—must be ready to make a giant investment. It means counseling and consoling and liturgy and child care and feminine liberation and sexuality and everything and anything that strengthens the bond. The bond of love. Because the bond is the important thing. Without the bond there is no sacrament. Without the sacrament there is no sign of God's love in the world. And without the sign of his love there is no hope.

NOTES

1. *Adversus Marcionem*, Lib. IV, c. 34; P.L. 2, 442.
2. *In Matthaeum Commentarii*, 14, 23; P.G. 10, 781.
3. *Divinae Institutiones*, Lib. VI, c. 23; P.L. 6, 719 and 720.
4. *Epistola 199, ad Amphilochium*, c. 35; P.G. 18, 1279.
5. *Epistola 217, ad Amphilochium*, c. 77; P.G. 18, 1310.
6. *Epistola 14, ad Bonifacium*, 2; P.L. 89, 525.
7. Denzinger-Bannwart, n. 397.
8. John T. Noonan, *Power To Dissolve* (Cambridge: Belknap Press, 1967), p. 80.
9. The first official document to refer to marriage as a sacrament was issued in 1184 by a local synod at Verona. See Denzinger-Bannwart, n. 402, and Edward Schillebeeckx, *Marriage: Human Reality and Saving Mystery* (New York: Sheed and Ward, 1965), p. 357.
10. Denzinger-Bannwart, n. 702.
11. Denzinger-Bannwart, n. 977.
12. See Victor J. Pospishil, *Divorce and Remarriage* (New York: Herder and Herder, 1967), pp. 62ff., and also Piet Franzen, "Divorce on the Ground of Adultery—The Council of Trent," in *The Future of*

Marriage As Institution, Volume 55 of the *Concilium* series, edited by Franz Böckle. An excellent review of the recent literature on indissolubility can be found in Richard A. McCormick's "Notes on Moral Theology," in *Theological Studies,* Vol. 32, pp. 107-122 and Vol. 33, pp. 91-100. A bibliography of the not quite so recent literature accompanies the interesting and scholarly article of William W. Bassett, "Divorce and Remarriage—The Catholic Search for a Pastoral Reconciliation," in *The American Ecclesiastical Review,* CLXII (1970), pp. 20-36 and 92-105.

13. *Poenitentiale Cummeani,* Canon 30. See Schmitz, H. J., *Die Bussbücher und die Bussdisciplin der Kirche,* I, Mainz 1883 and Graz 1958, p. 649. See also *Poenitentiale Cummeani,* Capitula Judiciorum, IX, 1; Schmitz, *op. cit.,* p. 660.

14. *Poenitentiale Theodori,* II, XIII, 4; Schmitz, *op. cit.,* p. 548.

15. *Poenitentiale Theodori,* II, XII, 23 and 24; Schmitz, *op. cit.,* p. 547.

16. See the *Monthly Vital Statistics Report* for May 1972, published by the U.S. Department of Health, Education and Welfare. An article entitled "More and More Broken Marriages" in *U.S. News and World Report,* August 14, 1972, noted that the divorce rate in the United States has risen 85% in the last ten years.

NOTES ON THE CONTRIBUTORS

REV. GEORGE W. MacRAE, S.J., Ph.D., is Stillman Professor of Roman Catholic Studies at the Harvard Divinity School and executive secretary of the Society of Biblical Literature. For several years he was co-editor of the journal *New Testament Abstracts.*

REV. BERNARD HÄRING, C.SS.R., is professor of theology at the Academia Alphonsiana in Rome. He is the author of numerous books, including *Church on the Move, Hope Is the Remedy,* and the three-volume *The Law of Christ.*

JOHN T. NOONAN, JR. is professor of law at the University of California Law School at Berkeley. He is the author of *Power To Dissolve: Lawyers and Marriages in the Courts of the Roman Curia* and has written extensively on questions of legal and ecclesiastical history.

VERNON J. BOURKE is professor of philosophy, specializing in ethics, at St. Louis University. Former president of the World Union of Catholic Philosophical Societies and the American Catholic Philosophical Association, he is associate editor of *American Journal of Jurisprudence* and author of *Ethics in Crisis, Will in Western Thought* and *History of Ethics.*

REV. JOHN CHARLES WYNN, author and editor of some six books on family life, is coordinator of The Graduate Study Program in Family Ministries for the member schools of The Rochester Center for Theological Studies. He is a certified marriage and family counselor in private practice, married, and the father of one son and two daughters.

HELEN McDANIEL, Ph.D., is a social worker and director of the Catholic Social Service agency of the Diocese of Columbus. She is a past member of the board of the National Conference of Catholic Charities and recently served on the 16-

151

member Cadre which designed the study and renewal program for the National Conference of Catholic Charities.

REV. ANDREW M. GREELEY is the Director of the Center for the Study of American Pluralism at the University of Chicago. He has written more than forty books, of which the most recent are *That Most Distressful Nation: The Taming of the American Irish*, *The Sinai Myth*, and a two-volume work on the sociology of religion: *The Denominational Society and Unsecular Man: The Persistence of Religion*. He is also editor of two new journals, *Ethnicity* and *Patterns in Religion and Behavior*.

KEVIN HERN, A.B., L.L.B., is a lawyer engaged in private practice in Boston. He is a graduate of Boston College and of Harvard Law School and has participated as counsel in a number of divorce cases. He has served on the councils of the Boston Bar Association and the American Arbitration Association (Boston), and is a Fellow of the American College of Trial Lawyers.

REV. EUGENE C. KENNEDY, M.M., is professor of psychology at Loyola University of Chicago, and the author of more than a dozen books, including *The Pain of Being Human* and *The Return to Man*. He also writes a bi-weekly newsletter, *You: The Quest for Spiritual and Emotional Fulfillment*.

REV. LAWRENCE G. WRENN is chief judge of the Tribunal of the Archdiocese of Hartford. He has been an annual lecturer on marriage procedures for several years at The Catholic University of America.